Foundations
of Engaged Scholarship

Foundations
of Engaged Scholarship

First Edition

Edited by W. Ross Bryan

Bassim Hamadeh, CEO and Publisher
Angela Schultz, Senior Field Acquisitions Editor
Michelle Piehl, Senior Project Editor
Abbey Hastings, Associate Production Editor
Emely Villavicencio, Senior Graphic Designer
Stephanie Kohl, Licensing Coordinator
Gustavo Youngberg, Interior Designer
Natalie Piccotti, Senior Marketing Manager
Kassie Graves, Vice President of Editorial
Jamie Giganti, Director of Academic Publishing

Cover image: Copyright © 2016 iStockphoto LP/Jacob Ammentorp Lund.

Printed in the United States of America.

ISBN: 978-1-5165-1115-0 (pbk) / 978-1-5165-1116-7 (br)

Contents

Contributors

Alexandra Gonzenbach Perkins, Instructor of Spanish, Department of Modern Languages and Classics, University of Alabama

Alexandra Huechteman, Research Assistant, Public Health Major/Biology Minor, University of Alabama Honors College

Anneliese Bolland, Assistant Research Scientist/Assistant Director, Institute for Social Science Research/Office for Undergraduate Research, University of Alabama

Brett Austin, Student, Aerospace Engineering Major, University of Alabama Honors College

Chad Tindol, Vice Chancellor for Risk and Compliance, Special Assistant to the Chancellor, and Deputy General Counsel, University of Alabama System

Charles Yeganian, Husband, Father, Citizen, New York, NY

Davis Jackson, Program Coordinator of 57 Miles, University of Alabama Honors College

Garrett Barnes, Student Facilitator, Nicaragua Clinical Experience, Food and Nutrition Major/Biology and Spanish Minor, University of Alabama

Jackson Knappen, Student Facilitator, Nicaragua Clinical Experience, Biology and Spanish Major, University of Alabama

Jessica Stershic, Research Assistant, Mechanical Engineering Major/Spanish Minor, University of Alabama Honors College

Joshua L. Fuller, Research Assistant, Criminal Justice Major/Public Policy Studies Minor, University of Alabama Honors College

Karson Holmes, Director of Tuscaloosa Rocketry Challenge, Mechanical Engineering Major on the STEM Path to the MBA, University of Alabama

Kim Bissell, Director of Undergraduate Research and Associate Dean for Research, University of Alabama

Leslie Parkins, Assistant Director, Office of Civic Engagement, Duke University

Robert E. Witt, Professor and President Emeritus, University of Alabama Honors College

Ryan Alverson, Assistant Professor, College of Education and Human Services, Northern Kentucky University

Foreword

THIS PROGRAM IS more than one of this institution's elite colleges or schools. It is a transformational experience.

During your time in this program, you will learn that asking the right questions is as important as knowing the right answers, that commitment and compassion are as important as competency, and that making a difference for others is as important as the success you personally achieve.

Thucydides said "we should remember that one man is much the same as another and that he is best who is trained in the severest school." This program is definitely not a "severe" school, but it will test, develop, and strengthen you. It will cause you to question ideas, values, society, the status quo, and yourself, and, in so doing, greatly enhance your horizons and your aspirations.

The essays in this book were written to help introduce you to an outstanding program and the experience before you.

Robert E. Witt
Professor and President Emeritus
University of Alabama

Introduction to Chapter 1

I HAVE HAD the pleasure of working with Joshua Fuller for the past couple of years as a student in my classroom and as my research assistant. In the following chapter we have tried to make a case for the how, why, and "so what" of education. It is a way for us to begin to question the philosophy of education, how we fund education in our society, and finally how much your education and educational opportunities should matter to you.

We ask large questions of educational institutions and the students who fill the seats within them. What is the purpose of you taking up a seat in your classroom? Is it to get a job? To become an enlightened citizen? Perhaps to make some connections with your fellow classmates, and the faculty and staff who can help you attain success in the future?

Additionally, we question access to education and how education plays a role in producing winners and losers in our society. This may sound harsh but education, more than any other institution, helps decide many fates of your fellow classmates.

We wrestle with all of these issues in the following chapter.

CHAPTER I

The Curious Case of Education

W. Ross Bryan, Joshua L. Fuller

IT IS IMPORTANT for us to begin with some simple, grand narrative questions to consider. The idea of education was not invented by your college and/or university, or by your K-12 experience. Many educational philosophers have discussed the notions and differences between "schooling," "learning," "indoctrination," "liberation", etc. For the purposes of this discussion, the chapter will seek to highlight "why" society educates and "how" we have constructed to school from K-16 and beyond, and give some framework to develop for the collective reader the relevance of modern education. More simply, we will try to answer the "so what" of education.

For young scholars, or more specifically, university students entering college/university, it is paramount that you decide why you have chosen to be in the seat you have taken in the modern university. It is my understanding that you do not want to be living in your parent's basement in four years. Trust that your folks do not want you to be there either. What do you hope to gain from this matriculation? Is it to obtain a job that will pay enough for you to take care of yourself in the way that you have become accustomed? Perhaps you are seeking to become an enlightened individual? (This is what all of your faculty like to think.) Or finally, and most simply, do you want to become socially mobile? Would you like to have a bigger house than your parental unit, a nicer car, a whiter picket fence to clearly delineate your and your neighbor's property? You will need this demarcation to hold your beloved pet and 2.4 children. This is a quick, simplistic way to view the purpose of education, and it is certainly focused on the individual.

If we were to move toward the collective reasoning on "why" we educate, would it be as simple? For instance, I had an old professor, Gerald Unks (professor emeritus, University of North Carolina at Chapel Hill), who used to tell his students that "we all pay for the undereducated and the miseducated." Dr. Unks told us we had to start with the understanding that "what we are really doing in education is deciding who has power in the next generation."

At the writing of this chapter, this remains a truth. It does not, however, fully explain why we have chosen to educate the way that we do as a collective. It is possible to follow the line of thought we have covered for the individual: so that people can get jobs; move society forward by developing new knowledge and passing it on; and finally, progress with a higher standard of living. This is not as easily done.

What happens if people do not want to be educated? This notion seems silly but should be explored. Not everyone can have a high paying job ... can they? What would we do if everyone in our society had a college degree? Would that work as it relates to the job market? My generation had a great pop culture icon whose character was in a movie titled *Caddyshack*. Ted Knight played a character named Judge Smails, who told his caddy on the golf course that if he could not afford to go to college and law school, it was acceptable because "the world needed ditch diggers too." How does this square with the American Dream and/or equal access to education? Quite simply it does not. Is education a product or a right that all citizens of our country should be afforded, or should it be viewed as a commodity that is available for individuals to purchase and benefit from? One thing is certain: education consumes a fair amount of societal resources. In fact, the United States spends more on primary and secondary public education than most developed nations. According to the National Center for Education Statistics (2015), the United States spends $620 *billion* on primary and secondary public education—6.4 percent of its GDP. Dividing that across all the public-school students in the United States, it amounts to roughly $12,300 per public school student/per year (OECD 2014; Fast Facts, n.d.).

Is education a public good or a private good? How do we view it? Does it enable and/or empower the individual or society? Should it be controlled by the federal government or the local school board? The simple answer is that we cannot decide as a macro- or microcommunity. It has vexed us since the founding of our nation. Again, as Dr. Unks tells us, we all philosophically "pay" for education; should we not all benefit from it?

There are many different ways to discuss the "why" of education. David Labaree (2000) lays out three main goals of education in our nation's history that can easily be framed as philosophies for our purposes:

> Grounded in this contradictory social context, the history of American education has been a tale of ambivalent goals and muddled outcomes. Like other major institutions in American society, education has come to be defined as an arena that

simultaneously promotes equality and adapts to inequality. Within schools, these contradictory purposes have translated into three distinguishable educational goals, each of which has exerted considerable impact without succeeding in eliminating the others. I call these goals democratic equality, social efficiency, and social mobility. (1997)

Labaree's goals give us a foothold to interrogate the "why" of education in a bit more detail. In his democratic equality philosophy, education is seen as a public good to benefit everyone. It is required that all citizens go through the process of schooling so that they may be competent citizens. In this model, school is compulsory (everyone must attend) and is meant to be equitable. "One argues that a democratic society cannot persist unless it prepares all of its young with equal care to take on full responsibilities of citizenship in a competent manner" (Labaree 1997, 42). This philosophy lends itself to the idea that everyone must have the same curriculum, delivered in the same way, at the same time. This takes us to the need for a unified curriculum. If we are all being prepared in the same way for citizenship, then we must all have the same material and delivery methods (pedagogy). An easy critique of this model would lead us to the position that not all of us learn in the same way; one could also argue that we may also have different areas that we would like to learn about, and maybe have different levels of interest and competencies. However, we must keep in mind that these are philosophies and not concrete steps to educating society.

In Labaree's social efficiency model, education is also seen as a public good. In this model, education is meant to fulfill job roles within society. If we need more widget factory workers, then we must create them in our schools. We will input widget factory knowledge into our curriculum, and students will be tracked into these pathways. In this way, curriculum is driven by the job market. This creates a socially efficient model for our students to follow. Students will be tested and tracked into job roles that they show competence in. The intent is not for Big Brother to have education as its tool; the intent is for us all to be working and able to earn a living. It is hard to dispute the fact that this philosophy lends itself to high-stakes testing, tracking of students, and ability groups. That standardized test you took in the fourth grade suddenly has much more significance. It may mean you are a line worker in the widget factory or perhaps have more potential and could possible supervise the factory. This would lead to stratified curriculum at some point. The factory line worker would have a different set of values placed on their education than the leadership of the factory. Either way, this seems a bit limiting of student's aspirations, although it certainly would be efficient (said the fascist ... wink).

The third philosophy is the one that is most closely tied to Judge Smails: social mobility. In this model, education is seen as a private good and goes to the highest bidder. Instead of curriculum becoming stratified, institutions become stratified. This stratification is generally based in cost to the consumer. Education will become commodified, and the quality will be dependent on what the student can afford. In this scenario, education will also become market driven in that institutions will change and bend to what the customer (student) wants. Meaning, as a professor I could theoretically sell my class to the students as "let me just take a few minutes and tell you how this freshman seminar will benefit your future self; you need this course and I am just the one to provide it for you. I promise you I will be funny and charming, and you will come out as a better student—just look at my ratemyprofessor.com surveys." We may be closer to this one than I originally thought. I think I just made myself queasy.

In classes, I get to this point and show a logo of Lexus and one of Toyota. Now, there is nothing wrong with a Toyota; I own two of them! I ask students if they would like the Toyota of education or the Lexus of education. Most students choose the Lexus version; the best part of this question is that the question is somewhat loaded. These hypothetical education companies are selling the same product, right? Toyota and Lexus are owned by the same company but the cars they make are not the same product. One is the luxury version, the upscale type, the high end; whatever it is, my initial thought is that we are basically talking about the same product. One just has more bells and whistles—a better sound system, leather interior, a moon roof, etc. If we are basically buying the same car or education, then why does one cost more than the other? In education it boils down to how society views this commodity. Is my degree from the University of North Carolina Asheville the same as one from Harvard? No. Why? Because society views it differently. And although I loved my classmates at UNC Ashville, maybe I would have had "better" classmates at Harvard. It is very possible that my having been educated at Harvard would have given me the ability to think differently or have power windows and a moon roof. Perhaps this is a good time to move to the "how" of education.

Here we meet Dr. Unks again. Remember when he said "what we are really doing in education is deciding who has power in the next generation"? We have discussed the "why" of education and we are going to now move onto the "how" of education. As a researcher and intellectual, I like to boil things down pretty quickly and then create a space to work within. Let us assume that Dr. Unks is right. How do we operationalize this within schools?

To understand how this power plays out in students' education, let's start with what we value in education. Here is a fact for you to ponder: it would be pretty easy for me to walk into any kindergarten classroom in this country and tell you which students would go on to college or university. I could do this and be about 95 percent accurate. I only need to know one piece of information that has nothing to do with achievement or ability. All I need to know is what the student's parents or caregivers do for a living. This is a bold statement, and I have never tested it, but I would be willing to bet I could do it. This untested fact does not make me feel good and warm. In fact, it makes me kind of queasy again. Social scientists refer to this as *social reproduction*, defined by Pierre Bourdeiu as "the reproduction of the structure of the relations of force between the classes" (Bourdieu and Passeron 1990, 11). The idea is that we reproduce the same pathways for our children that we had. Being socially mobile is very difficult and does not happen often; is it even possible? Of course! However, it takes a tremendous amount of resources, hard work, and luck to do it.

What implicit and explicit messages are we sending and receiving about education on a very surface level? Are these messages laden with societal values? Meaning, as it relates to education and how we educate, what do *we* value? Specifically, how do we fund public schools? In the private realm, are there "good" schools and "better" schools? If you attended a public or a private school in your home town, I would be willing to bet you could give me a pretty good rundown on the best to worst schools both public and private. What is this calculation based on? Is it the physical building and quality of books within the school? Is it the average income of the school's teachers and administrators? Perhaps how good their football team is? Or maybe the achievement level of the students within the school? Would it surprise you to know that we spend different amounts on student's education based on where they live? There is a simple formula that is the basis for how public schools are funded nationally. It sometimes is supplemented by states and local governments but the fundamental formula is called Per Pupil Expenditure (PPE), and it is as follows: tax base multiplied by the tax rate divided by the number of pupils in the district. Jonathan Kozol (1991) dedicated a whole book to this notion, titled *Savage Inequalities*. He did a masterful job of highlighting the differences in public school funding, citing examples from around the country using districts adjacent to each other. This is a larger issue that can be teased out at another time but the relevance to this project is the values we convey to our students when we see that society spends different dollar amounts on their education. Do we value some students more than others? Do we invest more in some students than others? Is this based on anything that they can control?

What about your education here, in college? Remember that 6.4 percent of the United States' GDP spent on education? Less than half of that—only 2.8 percent—is spent on postsecondary education, and most of that is delivered in the form of Pell and research grants (OECD 2014). General appropriations for colleges and universities come from state and local governments, and across the nation these bodies have steadily reduced their funding by varying degrees. In response, most colleges and universities have resorted to raising tuition costs to compensate for these losses, shifting a higher financial burden to the students these institutions serve. In the past ten years alone, postsecondary funding from student tuition has increased by 10 percent (SHEEO 2016). Why exactly have states reduced funding to higher education? Most research on the issue so far points to a sluggish recovery from the Great Recession; an ever-increasing number of college students to support (i.e., states must stretch the same dollars across more students); and states' requirement to keep a balanced budget, which becomes increasingly harder with less tax revenue to support state agencies and programs (Oliff et al. 2013).

What does this mean for higher education in regards to David Labaree's models of education? As colleges and universities continue increasing tuition costs to cover their spending, higher education will continue to become more and more of a private good, in line with Labaree's social mobility model. Without restating what has already been said about the social mobility model, one might predict that, in order to maintain prominence, institutions of higher education would target students with both the deepest pocketbooks and the best exam scores. In studying the socioeconomic gaps that already exist within higher education, Anthony Carnavale found that "among the most highly qualified students (the top testing 25 percent), the kids from the top socioeconomic group go to four-year colleges at almost twice the rate of equally qualified kids from the bottom socioeconomic quartile" (Oliff et al. 2013). Would we consider this fair, or equitable? Should two students, equal in every regard except for household income, be given different academic opportunities simply because one of them is able to pay more for a degree from the university they have both applied to? Is this the direction that we as a society wish to take our higher education? These are some of the questions that you as a college student might want ask yourself during your time at such an institution.

Let us look at two ends of a spectrum: Illinois and New York. As it stands during the time of this chapter's writing, the Illinois governor and legislature remain in a months-long partisan stalemate, refusing to pass a budget for political reasons that go beyond just higher education. However, because of this lack of cooperation, public universities in Illinois have closed down for days at a time, cancelled spring break vacations, and had students shower in gyms—on account of hot water not being available in the residence halls. All of these horrors have been committed in attempts to save enough money to survive another academic year without guaranteed state-allocated funding for higher education, attempts that have a lot of universities "getting ready to walk off the cliff" (Seltzer 2016; Rhodes 2017).

The story in New York, however, is much different. In April of 2017, New York governor Andrew Cuomo signed into law a bill that will make public college tuition free for all in-state students whose families make under $125,000 annually (Spector 2017). At first glance, this sounds like an incredible step in focusing higher education as a public good, does it not? Totaling over sixty campuses and four hundred thousand students, New York's public university system—City University of New York (CUNY) and State University of New York (SUNY)—is the largest in the country (Spector 2017). It turns out that, as with everything in life, one must read the fine print. The new plan, entitled the Excelsior Scholarship, guarantees a full tuition on two conditions—one, that students attend school full time and graduate in the typical time frame that one's degree is held to (two or four years); and two, that students spend a year in New York for every year they received the Excelsior Scholarship (Chen 2017). While many see these conditions as fair for up to four years of free tuition at face value, several communities cite these as impediments to the goals of the scholarship. In examining some of the Excelsior program's fine print, it becomes clear that this is not simply a plan for "free college" for everyone in New York, and several aspects of the scholarship will actually hinder higher education efforts.

According to the Governor's office, only 39 percent of students in four-year universities attain their degree on time. At two-year colleges, the number is 8.5 percent (New York State 2017). The full-time student requirement for the scholarship is said to address that by improving graduation rates and cutting student debt at the same time. In the same month that Governor Cuomo released his plan for the Excelsior Scholarship, however, a new study by David J. Deming found the exact opposite of his claim to be the case—money spent on institutional expenditures such as smaller class sizes, better faculty and counseling services increases college enrollment and completion, while tuition cuts for students result in very little, if any, increases (Deming 2016). Additionally, while New York's public education system already offers some of the lowest rates for in-state tuition in the country, nontuition expenses such as room and board, dining, and other fees amount to as much as two and three times as much as the cost of tuition, and the Excelsior Scholarship offers no assistance to students covering these costs (Friedman 2017). Excelsior has been marketed as a tool for middle-class families, and aptly so. The scholarship is a "last dollar" program, meaning that it only kicks in money after Pell grants and other financial aid packages are used, rendering many low-income students ineligible. Some point to existing programs like ASAP, a program within CUNY schools that offers many of the resources encouraged by the aforementioned Deming study, as a more appropriate target of increased funding. On the implications of Excelsior, former SUNY chancellor Johnstone remarked, "It will help a slice of middle-class students, but it's only a slice" (Chen 2017).

For the postgraduation residency requirement, the state plans to enforce it by transforming the scholarship into a loan charged to the student. According to the state's Department of Labor, 3.5 million jobs statewide are going to require associate's degrees or higher by 2024 (New York State 2017). Additionally, 80–90 percent of CUNY and SUNY graduates are already reported to remain in the state for work (Chen 2017; Webber 2017). One of the most vocal critics, however, Sara Goldrick-Rab, calls the residency requirement bad public policy, noting that other states like Tennessee that have begun to offer free tuition in public colleges have not included these types of caveats nor have they suffered because of it. Further, the requirement has the potential to reduce mobility if a recent grad cannot find a job in the state yet is offered a quality job elsewhere (Campanile 2017; Goldrick-Rab 2017). At a time when New York just marked a yearly net migration loss of 73,000, one might ask if there is indeed a correlation between the population decrease and the new scholarship requirement, which was not originally part of the proposal (Associated Press 2017; Webber 2017). Regardless of the intent, this residency requirement is a form of state protectionism, meaning the state of New York is, in effect, leveraging education against the market interests of itself. To go back to our widget factory metaphor earlier, it appears that New York needs more of its widget factory workers staying in the state, so they are offering to pay for the education one is required to have to make widgets. If David Labaree's second education philosophy, social efficiency, was not clear before, allow New York's residency requirement to the Excelsior Scholarship to serve as a real-time example.

While there is plenty of room for debate between the fine lines of the Excelsior Scholarship program, it cannot go without saying that the state of New York has taken an incredible step in providing public higher education at a scale greater than any state before it. CUNY and SUNY campuses are expecting to see increases in enrollment as soon as the program came into effect in the fall of 2017, and many project other states to follow in the footsteps of this New York model. This book is being written at the same time as these debates are occurring, so we are unable to remark on how it has played out thus far. However, we will be eagerly watching the program and the developments it provides to public education at the secondary level.

As consumers of higher education, students seemingly have more control of their educational dollars with regard to where and how they are spent. For the first time in many of their experiences they choose where to attend. However, this decision is based on many factors that are not very far from the democratic equality, social efficiency, and social mobility philosophies. To revisit a common thematic question, why are you here?

Again, we see this complicated by the idea of funding. Colleges and universities are not immune from the funding bug. In fact, institutions of higher education are arguably more affected by funding models. The Per Pupil Expenditure formula is not in play, but state appropriations, merit and needs-based scholarships, and access to opportunities certainly are. As an academic, I think that the three crown jewels of student satisfaction in their college choice are housing facilities, dining facilities/options, and recreation facilities (all in the student life realm). This fact does not keep me warm at night, but I understand that feeling at home and connected to their context is perhaps more important to incoming students than quality of instruction and/or faculty. Research tells us tells us that a sense of belonging is paramount to success in higher education (Alverson 2015; chapter 3 of this project).

How do these facts help us better understand how we educate in K–16? To better explain, I will draw on the concept of cultural capital (Bourdieu 1977). Bourdieu gives us this notion of cultural capital to use as a way to explain how we educate. As a reminder, this is directly tied to the "why" of education and the philosophies we discussed in the first part of this chapter.

For this argument, think about cultural capital as something you carry around in your pocket. You use this capital multiple times a day to negotiate power and purchase things you want or need within your context. This concept can also be understood formulaically:

Social Capital + Economic Capital = Cultural Capital

Social capital can be defined as who you know, or what societal contacts you have. Have you ever gotten a job because you knew someone who worked at the company? Other things such as race, class, gender, socioeconomic status, and sexual orientation/preference/identity can function as social capital that give you contextual power and/or influence. Bourdieu warns us that these forms of capital are contingent upon context, meaning that any of these forms of capital matter only in particular ways in particular places. For example, as the professor of a class, I have a fair amount of capital and can give some of that to my students as it relates to class, our institution of higher education, or simply providing a reference. My capital, or the capital that my students may take from me, is less than if we were in a different context or if they needed my influence/power to help them get a loan to buy a new car. Banks and loan officers do not necessarily care if your professor thinks you are intellectually in the top 5 percent of the class.

Economic capital is a bit more simply defined. It is currency, dollars, rubles, chickens, euros—anything that can be traded or bartered with to gain something. One can certainly have a tremendous amount of economic capital and very little social capital, thusly lowering one's cultural capital (reminder of formula: Social + Economic = Cultural).

Cultural capital is relevant to this discussion because this is the way we negotiate power in society. I would also argue that this is the primary way that we educate. As educators, we are providing students with opportunities to gain capital. Society has set up this structure for students to take advantage of "opportunities" so that they may "bank" their cultural capital (Freiere 1972). Students then use this capital to navigate their educational contexts. The chief piece of capital in and out of the classroom is grades; this subject is too large to enter into in this chapter but think, for a moment, how powerful a grade is to you. A pointed example is the significance of your standardized test score for college entry. A strong ACT or SAT score is very powerful and functions as capital within the context of higher education institutions; but as a reminder from Bourdieu, it would not matter much in my weekly pick-up basketball game. However, your ACT/SAT test scores along with your GPA had significant impact on where you chose to attend, who you were going to attend with, and how much you were going to have to pay for this opportunity. While it may seem simplistic to funnel all of the "how" of education to this one concept, it is an elegantly basic way to think of it. Take a moment and think about how much this one concept matters in education, particularly if you keep in the front of your mind that what we are really doing in education is deciding who has power in the next generation.

In the coming pages, we will expand on how we educate by using other examples, but this is the most important one. For instance, why are you in the seat you are in right now? As far as I understand the purpose of this project, your professor wants you to begin thinking about grand narrative questions to consider while you matriculate. Your professor wants you to be exposed to foundational ideas and toil with them. Once you have developed your opinion on these large questions, you can begin to take on other questions, and develop your own thoughts and critique.

We have discussed the "why" of education and mapped to "how" this is actualized in K–16 education. Some of these philosophies are in direct contradiction with each other as well as the ideas concerning how education gets played out in society. How can we explain this phenomenon to ourselves and, most importantly, the students who are receiving our educational efforts? We have a very hard time agreeing on the overall purpose of education in American society; is it any wonder that there are huge inequalities in how education is enacted? For a better understanding of the next step in this thought exercise, we will move to answering the "so what" of education. It will not illuminate some magical answer, far from it, but we may make more sense of education and why it should matter so much to us.

Education has historically been seen as the great equalizer of societal ills (Unks, 2000). It has been called on to rid us of isms, inequalities, and injustices. While I am not quite sure how fair it is to put this on education's shoulders, teachers and federal, state, and local school administrators have been trying to address various and sundry movements for over a hundred years. The Russians launched Sputnik, and thus began the space race. Education will catch us up and we will beat them. Racism has become a societal anchor? Education can fix that! Japanese car doors close better than ours? Our nation (and our schools) must be at risk (A Nation at Risk, 1983). We need to fix our schools—right now!

The very first text I was required to read as a doctoral student was John Willinsky's 1998 book titled *Learning to Divide the World: Education at Empire's End*. It was a comprehensive way to discuss why the philosophy and actualization of education matters to a society. In his work, Willinsky goes to great lengths to show that the Western notion of education is rooted in imperialism and colonialism, to show that this historical indoctrination has given educators the opportunity to create the purpose, the result, and the societal mattering of education. Willinsky encapsulates it this way:

> To establish the degree to which our current ideas of education may have been influenced by the global forces of imperialism, I lay out, in the following three historical chapters, the different ways in which imperialism was bent on taking a knowing possession of the world, on setting that world on public display for the edification of the West, and on developing the principal forms of schooling that might serve both colonial state and colonized native. (2000, 19)

When I discuss this piece of Willinsky's text in class, I always make a big show of drawing out precisely how I do this in the classroom, because educators remain implicated in this system. As a teacher I always spend the first day of class selling myself and this syllabus that is in front the student. I tell some jokes, tell them about me and my background/experience, discuss why this course (which I refer to as the greatest class ever) will benefit them and their future selves. I casually ask them what they would like to discuss in the course and make a grand show of saying (in the most benevolent manner) "I know what I think about this subject and how it relates to the world we live in, but I am most concerned about what YOU think" (taking knowledge). I then write down their thoughts and concerns, and go back to my office to weave their wants, needs, and ideas into the fabric of the course. In the very next class, I present them with an updated syllabus filled with their thoughts and ideas on what we will cover throughout the semester (public display for edification). I convince them that I am a benevolent educator who simply wants to make the world a better place by sharing in some discourse (serving the colonizer). Now, gentle reader, am I a bad guy? I don't think of myself as a bad professor, but I think Dr. Seuss would have a field day with me! It seems Grinchy in some ways, doesn't it? If education tried to extract itself from this imperialist model, how would we do it? What would we have to do? Foucault (1979) warns us that we need to at the very least examine where and how students sit, the time allotted to lessons, how non adherence to school is played out, and how the curriculum is developed and who it benefits from it. Conversely, don't we need order? Don't we all benefit from a shared notion of what and how school is articulated? Shouldn't we all learn in the same way, or at least learn the same type of stuff? What about the Great Books? Are they all of a sudden not so great anymore?

Upon closer examination, my role is to create content on what I know; dress it up, and make it pretty and wanted by the students; convince them that it will benefit them in some way; and then ultimately sell it to them. Certainly, a cynical way to look at education, but put this scenario back in the Willinsky model in K–16 education. It hits all the notes of imperialism, doesn't it? I am the colonizer and you are the colonized. I am creating little Rossites to go out and make the world a better place. Right?

What is "right" is not on my side. My daughter is six years old and understands enough of the world to relate to the good versus evil calculations. As college students, you all understand that this calculation can sometimes be very complicated. Are we sometimes complicit in really rotten and awful things? Of course we are. Life is complicated. Example: Is Darth Vader a bad guy? He is not a bad guy in the beginning or at the end, right? Who decides what good and bad is? More explicitly, who decides good and bad classes? Good and bad schools? Good and bad professors? Is my worth as a professor simply about how popular I am on ratemyprofessor.com or the college's satisfaction surveys given out at the end of the term? Do we value my entertainment and joke quality more than actual transfer of knowledge to the student? (Don't answer that one.)

In part, Willinsky is interrogating the idea of power and control of curriculum. If we take a step back and look at education in totality, we have to ask ourselves an additional question, which is "who decides what we learn and how we learn it." This is not the same as the "why," "how," and "so what" of education; it is related but slightly different. Who decides what we learn and what truth is? What is the difference in truth and knowledge? In Philosophy 101 we learn that there may be a big *T* truth and a little *t* truth. We find out that truth is subjective and can certainly be manipulated or massaged. Our role in education is to pursue truth in all forms. However, who is pushing truth and, perhaps more importantly, who's ideology is being promoted? Remember, controlling education is tremendously powerful.

Gerald Unks discusses the way schools are set up as a factory:

> The model that emerged as "the ideal" was not based on any psychological knowledge or established educational philosophy. The ideal school was based on a model borrowed from business and industry—the factory. Much that goes on in schools—the division of educational task into twelve "grades," the division of the school day into periods, the ringing bells, the system of quality control (A, B, C, D, F), the idea that everyone in the class should be working on the same material at the same time and at the

> same rate—all can be explained as remnants of the decision to
> base American schools on the factory model. (2000, 100)

Are students made in America fine motor vehicles? This notion that once students travel through the assembly line, gaining valuable skills and knowledge as they go through the factory is ridiculous. Yet, we are bound by this idea that after having gone through this machination process, competent and engaged citizens pop out at the end ready for the showroom floor. My old professor Dr. Unks (2000, 101) puts a fine point on how our factory model of schooling has worked historically: "Most college students will admit that they were never really challenged in high school. Twenty-five percent of our population is functionally illiterate. At least 15 percent have never been challenged by the school to work up to full capacity simply because the mold was no challenge for them. What industry, other than publicly funded bureaucracy, peopled by mindless ninnies, could stay in operation with a 40 percent rate of failure?"

This seems a bit harsh but these numbers are backed up by current research and reporting. The Literacy Project (Staggering Illiteracy, n.d.) reports that 50 percent of adults in our country can't read a book at an eighth-grade level, 45 million are functionally illiterate and read below a fifth-grade level, 44 percent of American adults do not read one book in a year, and six out ten household do not buy a single book in a year. These numbers are staggering and highlight the failings of how we have actualized schooling in our communities.

Who has built the factory and what product should we expect to see as an output? In "Ideology and the Ideological State Apparatus" (Althusser, 1971), the reader is presented with a framework to better understand society and societal power dissemination. Althusser presents the reader with pillars or tools used by the state to promote or push ideology; he calls them Ideological State Apparatus (religious, educational, family, legal, political, communications, and cultural). Althusser posits that the ideological state apparatus define and qualify social order. If we were to define what being an American is, we could start with an examination of the ideological state apparatus and how they have helped construct this notion of "Americanism." Among these, he lists education as perhaps the "dominant Ideological State Apparatus" (104). Althusser describes the educational ISA as so powerful because it is the premiere way for societal power to be reproduced.

> It takes children from every class at infant-school age, and
> then for years, the years in which the child is most 'vulnerable',

squeezed between the family State apparatus and the educational State Apparatus, it drums into them, whether it uses old or new methods, a certain amount of 'know-how' wrapped in the ruling ideology (French, arithmetic, natural history, the sciences, literature) or simply the ruling ideology in its pure state (ethics, civic instruction, philosophy). (104)

The educational state apparatus and its presentation is not meant to bog down our conversation; I include it to simply put forth the idea that education is controlled by ideology, and that the ruling class controls that ideology and will use education to reproduce itself and the structures that benefit it. We could have discussed this in the beginning of this chapter with the "why" of education, but that would have been a little soon to discuss class struggle and "social reproduction". However, it does help us get deeper into the "so what" of education.

The following chapters will, hopefully, illuminate and examine other foundational pieces of how education works and the purpose of education benefits you and society at large.

Works Cited

Althusser, L. (1971). Ideology and ideological state apparatuses (Notes towards an investigation). In Lenin and philosophy, and other essays (pp. 127–86). New York, NY: Monthly Review Press.

Associated Press. (2017, March 24). Census: More people leaving New York State. *U.S. News & World Report*. Retrieved from https://www.usnews.com/news/best-states/new-york/articles/2017-03-24/census-more-people-leaving-new-york-state

Bourdieu, P. (1977). *Outline of a theory of practice* (Cambridge studies in social anthropology, 16). Cambridge, UK: Cambridge University Press.

Bourdieu, P., & Passeron, J. (1990). *Reproduction in education, society and culture* (2nd ed.). London, UK: SAGE Publications.

Campanile, C. (2017, April 11). Cuomo's free tuition program comes with a major catch. *New York Post*. Retrieved from http://nypost.com/2017/04/11/cuomos-free-tuition-program-comes-with-a-major-catch/

Chen, D. W. (2017, April 11). New York's free-tuition program will help traditional, but not typical, students. *The New York Times*. Retrieved from https://www.nytimes.com/2017/04/11/nyregion/new-yorks-free-tuition-program-will-help-traditional-but-not-typical-students.html?_r=0

Deming, D. (2016, November). *The impact of price and spending subsidies on US post-secondary attainment*. In 2016 Fall Conference: The Role of Research in Making Government More Effective. Appam.

Fast facts: Elementary and secondary expenditures. (n.d.). *National Center for Educational Statistics.* Retrieved April 09, 2017 from https://nces.ed.gov/fastfacts/display.asp?id=66

Foucault, M. (1979). *Discipline and punish: The birth of the prison.* New York: Vintage Books.

Freire, P. (1972). *Pedagogy of the oppressed.* New York, NY: Herder and Herder.

Friedman, Z. (2017, February 06). Why New York's "tuition-free" college is not exactly free. *Forbes.* Retrieved from https://www.forbes.com/sites/zackfriedman/2017/02/06/college-free-no-student-loan/#49e9eaaa5960

Goldrick-Rab, S. (2017, April 11). Dear Jimmy: Making "Free College" Pay in New York. *Medium.* Retrieved from https://medium.com/@saragoldrickrab/dear-jimmy-making-free-college-pay-in-new-york-f6ba6696e430

New York State. (2017, January 11). *Governor Cuomo presents 1st proposal of 2017 State of the State: Making college tuition-free for New York's middle class families.* Retrieved from https://www.governor.ny.gov/news/governor-cuomo-presents-1st-proposal-2017-state-state-making-college-tuition-free-new-york-s

Jaschik, S. (2017, April 10). New York adopts free tuition. *Inside Higher Ed.* Retrieved from https://www.insidehighered.com/news/2017/04/10/new-york-state-reaches-deal-provide-free-tuition-suny-and-cuny-students

Kozol, J. (1991). Savage inequalities: Children in America's schools. New York: Crown Pub.

Labaree, D. F. (2000). No exit: Public education as an inescapably public good. In L. Cuban & D. Shipps (Eds.), *Reconstructing the common good in education: Coping with intractable American dilemmas* (pp. 110–129). Stanford: Stanford University Press.

National Center for Education Statistics. (2015). Average undergraduate tuition and fees and room and board rates charged for full-time students in degree-granting postsecondary institutions, by control and level of institution and state or jurisdiction: 2013–14 and 2014–15. Retrieved from https://nces.ed.gov/programs/digest/d15/tables/dt15_330.20.asp?current=yes

OECD. (2014). *Education at a glance 2014: OECD indicators.* Paris, France: OECD Publishing. DOI: http://dx.doi.org/10.1787/eag-2014-en

Oliff, P., Palacios, V., Johnson, I., & Leachman, M. (2013, March 19). *Recent deep state higher education cuts may harm students and the economy for years to come.* Retrieved from Center on Budget and Policy Priorities website: http://sbba4he.org/wp-content/uploads/2013/04/CBPP_Higher_ED_3-19-13sfp.pdf

Rhodes, D. (2017, March 18). Illinois regional universities toil through state budget standoff. *The Chicago Tribune.* Retrieved from http://www.chicagotribune.com/news/local/breaking/ct-budget-crisis-regional-universities-20170316-story.html

Seltzer, R. (2016, October 5). "Nail in the coffin" for Chicago State? *Inside Higher Ed.* Retrieved from https://www.insidehighered.com/news/2016/10/05/chicago-state-struggles-under-questions-enrollment-finance-leadership

SHEEO (State Higher Education Executive Officers Association). (2016). *Distribution of Funding Sources* [Graph illustration].

Spector, J. (2017, April 10). Free college tuition for middle class students? N.Y. lawmakers vote yes. *USA Today.* Retrieved from https://www.usatoday.com/story/news/2017/04/10/new-york-free-college-tuition-middle-class-students-suny/100276448/

Staggering illiteracy statistics. (n.d.). Retrieved from Literacy Project Foundation website: http://literacyprojectfoundation.org/community/statistics/

United States. National Commission on Excellence in Education. (1983). A nation at risk: the imperative for educational reform: a report to the Nation and the Secretary of Education, United States Department of Education. Washington, D.C.: The Commission: [Supt. of Docs., U.S. G.P.O. distributor].

Unks, G. (2000). *Schooling in America: Cases, studies and comment.* Dubuque, IA: Kendall/Hunt.

Webber, D. (2017, April 13). This U.S. state's free college plan isn't all it's cracked up to be. *Fortune.* Retrieved from http://fortune.com/2017/04/13/free-college-tuition-new-york-excelsior-scholarship-pay-education-bill/

Willinsky, J. (2000). *Learning to divide the world: Education at empire's end.* Minneapolis: University of Minnesota Press.

Young Invincibles (2016). *2016 State Report Cards.* Retrieved from https://www.luminafoundation.org/files/resources/yi-state-report-cards-2016.pdf

Introduction to Chapter 2

IT IS MY hope that you have already begun to develop a place in your new community at your college or university. You have already met several people who have told you that you must become engaged or involved while you are in college. In fact, there are probably three or four people who you have met with this week who are compensated in some way to ensure that you are plugged into your new environment. It is important, we want you to feel welcome, we want you to know about the resources available to you here at good old College University!

Dr. Alverson has done a great deal of research on how a sense of belonging has positive, long lasting effects on a student. You will have better grades, feel at home faster, and begin to construct a narrative for yourself that always includes your home institution. Which, ideally, will help you make a good choice in giving back to your home institution at some point so others can have the same opportunities that you did.

The benefits of feeling like you belong in your new community of scholars is of the utmost importance. Dr. Alverson will explain why in the following chapter.

CHAPTER 2

Belongingness in Education

A Critical Institutional Issue Examined from a Psychosocial Perspective

Ryan Alverson

Introduction

FEELING INCLUDED AND valued in the school environment is something that most of us yearn to experience. We have all been in a classroom, at some time or another, in which we felt left out or disconnected from the other students and teacher. Perhaps we have felt alienated in a particular elementary or middle school classroom. I moved around a lot as a young child, and remember that entering a new classroom in the middle of the school year was always an intimidating process and often left painful memories. Sometimes, I would feel awkward and scared during those times when other students did not take the initiative to welcome me or when the teacher did not go out of the way to ease my transition. These experiences would sometimes hamper my learning or would place me in a situation in which I could not function at the best of my ability. In college, I am sure that most of us have sat in a large lecture hall thinking that the professor does not even realize that we exist. We might as well just be another number out of a hundred rather than a breathing and thinking human being. Now, let's contrast these experiences by thinking back to a particularly happy and meaningful school year. My guess is that our reflections would include feelings that we matter and make a difference. These feelings were probably supported by a close group of classmates or friends that had our back, as well as a teacher who cared, supported, and challenged us to our fullest potential. I would venture to guess that we were most engaged in these classes rather than the former. These are the types of school experiences that make our education meaningful and that we desire.

This chapter examines the critical issue of belongingness in education from a psychosocial standpoint. Belongingness, or sense of belonging, is the sense that one believes they "fit in" and are a valued member of the school community. *Psychosocial* should not be confused with Erikson's psychosocial theory of development (Erikson 1993) or a psychoanalytic view, but rather it is situated in the context of the psychological processes of the learner and the social processes that support the psychological processes of learners. Before we examine belongingness, let us look at how this issue fits into the larger picture of education. One could argue that education, as Horace Mann posits, is the "great equalizer of the conditions of men" (Cremin 1957). In this sense, education is the mechanism by which we gain equal footing in the world, but this can only be accomplished when education is deployed in a universal manner. Universal education is necessary for society to function well, yet one could argue that there are roadblocks and obstacles to universal education within the confines of the single classroom and at the institutional level. One way of examining the concept of universal education is to look at the inequalities that exist with respect to access to education. Or, as this chapter attempts to do, we can look at the fundamental psychological processes of the learner and educator, and how certain social processes support or fail to support these psychological processes within the school and classroom. By doing this, one can see how inherent inequalities sometimes exist within the confines of the learning environment that run counter to the idea of universal education. In this way, we can examine the idea of universal access to education, at a microsystemic level, rather than a macro level. Specifically, this chapter examines the psychological perceptions of believing that one is an integral part of the educational process, and the psychological processes and social support systems put in place by the educator and larger institution that help to promote the perceptions of the individuals who are being educated. These perceptions play an important role in the integration of students within the particular institution of education on both academic and social levels (Tinto 1975). Therefore, this chapter views fundamental differences in psychological processing of the learner and educator as a foundation on which unequal educational experiences are built. These unequal educational experiences work against the idea of belongingness.

You may be wondering, why should we examine inequalities in educational experiences and their roots in perceptual differences in students and educators? It is important because if we do not feel integrated into the educational community, then we will not be engaged and doing meaningful work. And, probably most importantly, if we do not feel integrated into the educational fabric of our school, and if we do not do all that we can to help other students feel the same, then what are we doing here?

Gaps in Educational Quality

One of the critical issues in education is the lack of equity. Equity, in this sense, refers to the differences in quality of education received by students. From a historical perspective, one can look to *Plessy v. Ferguson* (Thomas 1996) and the decades that followed to inform one's knowledge regarding equal education for all. One can also look to economic issues and funding differences that exist throughout the different states and localities in this country to see how access to education is affected. This chapter proposes that a lack of equity in education can also stem from differences in the fundamental ways that people process and perceive information. It's no secret that we live in a diverse world, and with diversity comes diverse thought.

This diversity in thought can be problematic in educational settings. Teachers approach education in a variety of ways, from their preferred way of teaching to their fundamental beliefs about what should be taught and how it should be taught. Furthermore, their basic underlying assumptions about the purpose of education come in a variety of shapes and sizes. Universals often exist within educational professionals, however, with respect to common principles of education, including the desire for all humans to experience a quality education and for pupils to use education in positive ways in their lives and in the lives of fellow persons. These common strands of altruistic thought are sometimes lost in the actual interactions that take place in educational settings, creating divides in the quality of education received by students due to the psychological and socioemotional perceptions of the individuals being educated. Finding ways to engage in positive interactions can be a struggle for students as well as teachers, especially as students transition into college from high school. As freshmen in college, we are often interacting in strange, new environments and among strange, new people. How do we find, or create, familiar and engaging relationships in our new college lives? This is something for which we should all be searching.

When examining the gap in quality of education resulting in the alienation of certain students, it's important to look at the pathology of this gap and alienation so possible solutions can be proposed to address these practices. In doing so, hopefully we can create a more inclusive body of students within whatever educational setting we are experiencing. The issue of not believing that one "fits in" the educational setting is one that affects students in many different educational institutions. When this type of thinking is assessed, it is often done so through student self-report measures. It is thinking that is experienced on the part of the student. The key question here is, why do some students think like this, that is, feel as if they don't belong in their school or educational institution? One possibility is rooted in the types of support systems, or more appropriately, lack of support, in place. Sometimes our interactions with peers and others in the educational setting work to make us, or others, feel left out. Tinto suggested that one's peer relationships in college are a critical component concerning their integration within the college experience (1987).

One could argue that perceptions of not "fitting in" boils down to lack of inclusion at the classroom and campus level. One headline in *The Northerner*, the independent student newspaper of Northern Kentucky University, read "Student: Lack of Inclusion is a 'Campus Problem'" (Manley 2016). This article highlighted a particular incident that occurred at the beginning of the fall 2016 semester on the Northern Kentucky University campus. Unknown posters (assumed to be students) posted "Welcome White Week" flyers in response to "Welcome Black Week" flyers. The "Welcome Black Week" flyers have been a means of advertising the various African American student groups on campus and the corresponding opening week activities in place that support the transition of students of color and other minority student groups on campus. Many students of color shared their feelings of being targeted (2016) and excluded on a campus that is supposed to stand counter to this type of activity. The university did condemn the flyers, and the general student body did hold meaningful discussions surrounding this incident, but the main point is that a student, or group of students, acted in a manner that was the polar opposite to what an inclusive community of support entails. This particular incident might be considered an extreme example of practices that create a culture of noninclusiveness, but many other microaggressions that students commit, however intentional or unintentional they may be, make for an unwelcoming experience for those students on the receiving end.

Disengagement and Withdrawal of Students

Gaps in educational quality often manifest in the disengagement and withdrawal of marginalized students. Disengagement and underachievement of students is related to poor perceptions of connectedness and belonging in school. These students have a hard time feeling that they belong and believing they are important members of the school community. There are many possible reasons that account for the sense of disconnectedness, low achievement, and, ultimately, disengagement and withdrawal of marginalized groups of students, but this chapter focuses on the relational factors within the educational setting as well as the perceptions of the educator and the types of support educators and others give within the educational setting.

Many students experience issues with integrating into the school community and eventually become disengaged and withdrawn (Newmann 1981; Finn 1989; Newmann 1992). It is "socially and psychologically valuable for people to work with and relate to one another as integrated, active participants, rather than in a withdrawn, passive manner" (Newmann 1981, 549). In contrast to withdrawn students, engaged students are "psychologically invested" in learning (Newmann 1992). This distinction highlights the gap among students in two different camps. In one camp we have the students who perceive that they fit in the school community well; therefore, they are engaged and more likely to be successful. In the other camp are the students who feel disconnected. This is a somewhat simplified and binary way of looking at integration of students in the school community, and there are surely many students that fall somewhere within a gray area. It is, however, important to look at the opposing sides of this gap to begin understanding the mechanisms that enable this gap to occur.

Racial and Gender Issues of Belongingness

Belongingness research dealing with race and ethnicity reveals several things. Regarding racial differences in belongingness, greater levels of attachment exist for students who attend school with higher proportions of their own race (Johnson, Crosnoe, and Elder 2001). One could argue that we are more comfortable around people of our own race; therefore, we feel like we fit in more with those who are similar to us. For those of us who have not been exposed to diverse environments before, we might tend to feel awkward or out of place when grouped with people with different backgrounds. One particular study found that early experiences of belongingness for first- and second-year Latino college students positively impacted their experiences by their third year, and those students who perceived a hostile racial climate were negatively impacted during their college experiences around integration within the college community (Hurtado and Carter 1997). In short, when we are comfortable and engaged in positive relationships with those around us, we benefit from these experiences and tend to do better in school. The opposite can happen when we do not feel supported or like we belong in a particular school setting. Research has also highlighted the positive relationship between sense of belonging in institutions of higher education, and persistence and commitment to the institution (Hausmann, Schofield, and

Woods 2007). This held true for both African American and white students at this particular institution, suggesting that the positive effects of perceiving that one belongs holds true among students of different races. One thing that we can take away from this is that when we think our classmates and teachers support us and value who we are, we will then try harder and perform better in school. When we feel left out, our academic work suffers. It makes sense that if we want to succeed and help others succeed, we should search for ways of fitting in and making sure that others fit in as well.

There is research that suggests a gender gap exists with respect to enrollment and achievement in the fields of math and science. Some literature argues that sense of belonging for women, especially in mathematics, may help women persist in their work as well as boosting their grades. This same research suggests that when females do not believe that they are naturally good at math, it can negatively impact their sense of belonging in math, but not so for males (Good, Rattan, and Dweck 2012). Research has also found that stereotypical things associated with computer science and found in a typical educational setting sway women away from experiencing the same sense of belonging as men do in the field of computer science (Cheryan et al. 2009). In this case, it was associated with women feeling that they did not have a place in computer science and therefore did not pursue it (2009). Simply put, the world of math and science is often built for men, and it is communicated to students in this way.

The Big Picture of the Problem

It's not so much *what* we teach or learn, necessarily, as it is *how* we teach it or learn it. What do these critical issues mean for how we interact with our fellow classmates? How do the perceptions of students and educators within the educational community work for or against the integration of everyone within this community? As students, we should strive to become a part of the educational experience as well as helping others to do the same. Essentially, we should strive to become well-informed citizens of the world with meaningful purpose. These are issues and questions that the remaining part of the chapter will address, and will hopefully shed some light on what it means for achievement and meaningful participation in the college experience.

Implicit Biases That Color Our Interactions

How we see the world affects everything that students and educators do, from instructing, learning, participating in class, and dealing with other humans. And, if our perceptions are colored with biases or preferences for certain people or things, then we can be communicating in ways that negatively impact other people. Take the research, for example, that points to lower enrollment of females in STEM related courses (Riegle-Crumb and King 2010; Sadler et al. 2012). Much of how we are socialized into what we believe about gender roles is communicated to us in ways that suggest females are better suited to other pursuits such as the home. Even though we may not discuss these things directly, the implicit ways in which we discuss them inside and outside the school setting affects us in real ways.

This section discusses some ways that educators with implicit biases are at fault in creating environments that are not as inclusive as they could be. A study at Yale (Gilliam et al. 2016) found that "because of implicit bias, teachers are spending too much time watching black boys and expecting the worst." This finding, coupled with the fact that there are a disproportionate number of Black boys being expelled and suspended in early education settings, highlights the growing need for interventions aimed at reducing implicit bias in educational settings (2016). Not only does implicit bias affect preschools, but it also happens at institutions of higher education. No educator is immune to it. Implicit biases, created through subconscious stereotypes, guide our interactions with people. These types of interactions in the classroom and educational institution can have negative effects where they may not be necessarily intended. Researchers at the University of Washington, Harvard University, and the University of Virginia have examined implicit biases and how this affects our perceptions of people who are different than us with respect to cultural differences and leads to discriminatory practices (Greenwald, McGhee, and Schwartz 1998). Through their work with Project Implicit, they have administered and validated an association test that measures our implicit biases. Anyone is free to take this test online. In a few short minutes, it reveals the implicit associations that all of us hold and might serve as a useful tool in examining our individual perceptions that could very well affect our interactions with our fellow students. All this being said, the problem lies not in the implicit associations that we have but in how we deal with these implicit associations on a daily basis. What can we do to overcome some of our own faulty thinking regarding our interactions with other peers, students, and professors?

The Effects of Deficit Thinking

Another orientation that educators adopt too often is a focus on perceived deficits of skills and knowledge (Gordon and Crabtree 2006). This runs parallel to the traditional psychological model of the last half century in which illnesses and other deviations from normality in thinking or health need to be "fixed." Teachers often focus on student weaknesses rather than on what students do well. Gordon calls this the "weakness trap" (2006). For most of our lives we have been exposed to this type of thinking and the language associated with this type of thinking. We have a natural tendency to focus on weaknesses because that is what we are used to experiencing. For example, think about the student who just doesn't cut it in class. She has a record of failures and can't seem to reach average or above-average mastery of the content. It would seem natural that the teacher would want to help this student learn what she doesn't know in order to pass the assessment or assignments and ultimately pass the course. The problem with this is that the teacher is not utilizing what this particular student is naturally good at, and this can lead to a state of helplessness and feelings of not being a part of the learning community on the part of the student. For all intents and purposes, we are promoting disengagement and alienating students when we do this.

We can also say the same thing from the perspective of the student. When we come across those courses or educational experiences that challenge us, it is easy to dismiss those things that we cannot do well naturally. This is not necessarily a bad thing, but it can be disheartening and make us feel defeated when we are required to do certain things but cannot seem to find ways of accomplishing them. Gordon and Crabtree would also argue that, in this case, we are not focusing on what we should be focusing on, which is our inherent talents (2006). When we work from a place of inherent talents—the traits that we are good at naturally—our work and accomplishments seem to flow with ease. When we work counter to this, works and accomplishments come much harder.

Antiprogressivism from a Psychological Viewpoint

One could also argue that antiprogressivism plays a part in pushing people who hold perspectives counter to the norm to the fringes. In this case, antiprogressivism means any practices that fail to consider the learner's psychological perspective, cultural beliefs and values, and other background information. By doing this, we are ignoring one's unique contributions to the learning process as well as failing to consider the ways that one learns best, which is to build from the foundation of knowledge and skills that a student brings to the table. This runs counter to what Dewey would consider to be the environments that allow us to thrive and grow (Dewey 2007). During the current education reform movement in primary and secondary schools that has been growing steadily for the last few decades (National Commission on Excellence in Education 1983; NCLB 2001), there is much examination and discussion around curriculum reform, with Common Core being the most recent topic of debate in schools. What these efforts highlight is a focus on the "what" is being taught versus the "how" or process of teaching and learning, and by ignoring the process, we are doing a disservice to learners and what they bring to the table in terms of cultural and cognitive contributions. Next, we will look at approaches to education that offer potential solutions to the issues surrounding lack of inclusiveness stemming from the educational processes that we have just discussed.

Educational Approaches That Promote Inclusiveness

Different perspectives exist as to how we can address the problem of the gap in quality of education. In the context of this chapter, there are three underlying themes that characterize these educational approaches, which offer promise in bridging this gap. These themes include mechanisms that support and enhance belongingness in the educational setting. The quality gap viewed through the issue of belongingness includes perceived differences in the degree to which students feel that they belong in the educational setting and are valued and respected members of the school community (Goodenow 1993). Positive psychology, especially well-being theory, is a second theme through which we can examine the gap in educational quality. This approach, as a whole, is a fundamental shift in how we view the educators and those who are being educated. The final theme discussed in this chapter involves putting the learner at the forefront of the educational process. There are different ways of handling all of these themes, or approaches, and a large part of the process has to do with the way the individuals with stakes in the process interact with one another and act as support mechanisms. We can then examine the means by which these support mechanisms are employed in the specific educational setting. Dewey would say that "we never educate directly, but indirectly by means of the environment. Whether we permit chance environments to do the work, or whether we design environments for the purpose makes a great difference. And any environment is a chance environment so far as its educative influence is concerned unless it has been deliberately regulated with reference to its educative effect (2004, 23).

Essentially, the themes as discussed in this context offer a more effective way of reaching everyone and making them feel included in the learning process, and help them to receive a comparable quality of education from a psychological viewpoint.

Being Deliberate about Inclusiveness

According to this perspective, we need to be deliberate in our design of the learning environment so that every individual is not only included in the learning process as a physical being but also as a psychological being with real contributions to be made to the educational environment. A key aspect of including each individual in the learning environment in this manner means that we form lasting and positive relationships with one another in the mutually beneficial endeavor of education. The literature on sense of belonging, or connectedness, as it is sometimes called, within the educational environment is often framed in the humanistic tradition. Some would argue that humans have an innate need to belong (Maslow 1954; Kohut 1984; Baumeister and Leary 1995). A review of the literature on attachment theory would suggest that we are actually born with the need to form relationships with those people closest to us as to have a secure base from which to take on our various pursuits in life (Bowlby 2008; Ainsworth 1979). These relationships must be positive and stable, with a mutual concern for the welfare of those involved (Baumeister and Leary 1995). Out of these perspectives arises the argument that those people in positions to do so must do everything that's possible and within their means to make sure others feel valued and included. This means that we work to form positive relationships in the school. We do this because we know from research that these relationships are critical mechanisms that underlie success in school.

Educational settings void of these critical relationships promote higher rates of absenteeism, lower self-regulation, less prosocial behavior, and higher rates of aggressive behavior in individuals (Alverson 2014; Baumeister et al. 2005; Twenge et al. 2007; Twenge et al. 2001). On the other hand, experiencing these types of positive relationships is related to achievement as measured by standardized test scores, academic self-efficacy, intrinsic motivation, and social acceptance (Alverson 2014; Freeman, Anderman, and Jensen 2007). Sense of belonging has been found to significantly predict grades and academic competence in college students when controlling for gender (Pittman and Richmond 2007).

The example at the beginning of the chapter discussed those times we felt particularly welcomed or unwelcomed in school. As students, we appreciate those times when our teachers try extra hard to make us feel welcomed and offer us the support that we need. It also helps when teachers take the time to personally meet with us outside of class to offer advice or help us with an assignment. It feels great when our teachers make us feel special. As students, it is nice to have that close-knit group of friends or classmates whom we can rely on for support. Perhaps we miss class on a particular day, and we need someone to fill us in on the day's agenda or notes. Sometimes our relationships with fellow students are strong enough that we become more than just classmates or organization members. These relationships become lasting and might have positive effects far into the future. Even those relationships or smaller interactions that don't extend beyond the scope of the school campus can impact us positively and for the better. The research makes it clear about the positive effects these types of relationships have on our academic and social success. We should all be thinking of ways to create a more inclusive, accepting, and welcoming school campus. Positive relationships are contagious, and it would serve us all well to do our part in developing and sustaining the types of relationships that enable all of us to feel like we belong here. We should also not assume that creating a more inclusive campus climate is beyond our responsibility. We can all play a part in effectuating belongingness, even if it requires us to move past our comfort zones.

Belongingness Within Other Frameworks

Other theorists include relational factors in their conceptualization of motivational frameworks. According to self-determination theory, we are motivated to succeed when we are autonomously directed, perceive that we are competent, and experience relatedness with others (Deci and Ryan 1985). This means that we need to strive to be self-directed learners and work so that others are able to do the same. Making others feel competent is also necessary, and we can do this by valuing their input and building on each other's success while also learning how to positively deal with failure in our lives. Finally, we need to find ways of relating to other people and building the positive relationships that allow this to happen. Simply put, when we sincerely work on building lasting, positive relationships, we focus on a critical component that helps to make others and us successful in school. And, when we build positive relationships, and promote competence and autonomy, we have greater intrinsic motivation and strive for challenges in our lives.

Contributions of Positive Psychology

Other theoretical frameworks within the realm of positive psychology examine the growth of humans in positive and healthy ways. Positive psychology focuses on what people do well rather than what we do poorly and aims to build people up rather than "fix" us (Seligman and Csikszentmihalyi 2014). It seeks to answer the questions of what makes life most worthwhile and how we can help people to flourish (2014). Seligman frames the various theories in terms of being oriented in experiences of the past, present, and future. For example, hope and optimism are examples of future-oriented theories in that hopeful and optimistic people are able to envision the future in positive ways. Well-being theory seems particularly suited to addressing the aforementioned issues of lack of inclusiveness and the lack of perceiving that one is a valued member of the educational setting. Well-being is a construct, and according to Seligman (2012), it has five elements, which can each be measured: positive emotion, engagement, relationships, meaning and purpose, and accomplishment (PERMA). The idea is that these elements can be increased in order to increase our well-being. In the context of this chapter, all of these elements (relationships being the obvious one) play important roles in the perception that one is well and flourishing, or growing to one's potential. Essentially, if we are supporting all of these elements at the classroom and institutional level, then we are working to close the equity gap.

Focusing on What We Do Well

In addition to building positive relationships, we should find ways of utilizing what we do best. "Above all, they [educators] should know how to utilize the surroundings, physical and social, that exist so as to extract from them all that they have to contribute to building up experiences that are worthwhile" (Dewey 2007, 15). One way of using all aspects of our surroundings is to rethink what we do from a strengths perspective. Earlier, this chapter highlighted the critical mistake of approaching education using a deficit-reduction model, or as Gordon and Crabtree would say, falling into the weakness trap (Gordon and Crabtree 2006). We have a natural tendency to seek out and recognize weaknesses, as in those skills and knowledge that fall below the "normal" levels we normally see. In the classroom, this translates to only recognizing those students who are not performing at the same levels as their peers and trying to bring those students up to speed with everyone else. The problem with this approach is that we tend to ignore what these students have to offer, which may be something valuable to the learning process. Let us turn this around to approach learning by focusing on what every individual in the educational environment does well naturally. The Gallup organization argues that we need to focus on students' inherent talents and then find ways of building on these talents so that they develop into strengths. This can be a difficult thing to do, especially when we're used to focusing on weaknesses. We also lack the language with which to discuss each other's strengths. Gallup has some suggestions for discussing our strengths, including a way to measure our inherent talents.

The Learner-Centered Educational Experience

One additional approach to promoting sense of belonging on campus is to construct our educational experiences around the unique contributions of each individual's background knowledge and inherent psychological functioning (Bransford, Brown, and Cocking 2000). We all have something to say and something to offer to our fellow students. We all have our own lives that we know about but that our classmates and professors do not necessarily know about us. All of our knowledge and skills, including our cultural experiences that have contributed to our knowledge, shaped who we are today. Not only do we need to recognize and use our own cultural contributions to who we are, but we need to accept one another for who we are and help to create a safe place for expressing our thoughts and ideas. By doing these things, we are working on establishing a learner-centered community within the educational environment (2000). Communities of learners in which all members feel safe and supported should be one of the main goals of our educational endeavors on campus.

Future Directions

We have discussed some of the critical issues regarding the integration versus nonintegrating of students from the reference of understanding the psychological mechanisms by which we feel like we belong and are a valuable member of the school community. By looking at the educational practices and support systems that promote inclusiveness or noninclusiveness in the classroom and larger institutional setting, we can begin to understand where we stand currently as well as some of the next steps that need to be taken. These next steps should be aligned with the practices of the members of our particular institution of higher learning, which will promote learning experiences that are meaningful, mind expanding, and ultimately exceptional. These exceptional learning experiences will, hopefully, help us to have a better understanding of ourselves and the world around us as well as helping us to improve our world.

The Learning Environment (What Students and Teachers Should be Doing)

Every facet of the institution—from the physical classroom to the psychological climate amongst faculty, administrators, and students—should stand to serve as the learning environment and foundation that supports learners in perceiving they are valued members of the learning community. Only then can the gap in educational quality begin to narrow. In the words of Dewey (2004), "it is the office of the school environment to balance the various elements in the social environment, and to see to it that each individual gets an opportunity to escape from the limitations of the social group in which he was born, and to come into living contact with a broader environment."

It is the responsibility of all of us to do these things. By not doing them, we are contributing to the very issues that we claim to oppose. By doing them, we are aligning ourselves with the mission of our institution.

Part of rethinking the learning environment involves rethinking what we have always done or the experiences to which we have always been exposed. So much of what we do involves trying to make people buy into our way of thinking or involves someone trying to get us to adopt their mode of thinking that we forget what it is that we find important and relevant to us. By doing the same thing we have always done, we limit our minds. By expanding our experiences around diverse thoughts and viewpoints, we expand our minds, which makes our learning more meaningful.

The Big Picture in Closing

What does all of this mean for students engaged in scholarship and service within higher education? Approaching education from the argument proposed in this chapter—narrowing the gap in quality of education by respecting and valuing everyone involved in the learning process and making sure all individuals perceive that they matter and belong—means that we are getting closer to universal education, maybe not exactly as Mann (1848) discussed it but from a psychosocial standpoint. The research tells us that a chief variable in achievement and success stems from the degree to which we feel that we belong. This should be one of our main goals, and we can all play a key part in fostering this goal.

As college students, particularly freshmen who are just beginning the journey of higher education, creating a campus in which all students feel like they belong is well within reach and should be at the top of our priority lists. Many students are concerned with making friends or joining a particular Greek or extracurricular organization, while some students may only be focused on getting good grades and maintaining a 4.0 grade point average during this time in school. For some students, academics is their life and consumes most of their time during the day. They eat, sleep, and breath it. Hopefully, this chapter makes it clear that these two, seemingly different, focuses in college do not have to be that different or separate after all. Creating positive relationships that make us feel like a valuable part of the higher education process, inside and outside of the classroom and campus, can work with our academic side to create something powerful. In order to do this, we must move beyond our zones of comfort and do everything we can to build the types of campus communities that are welcoming and supportive of all students. These two areas of our lives can actually complement one another and act to make our experiences in school much better than if they were treated as separate parts of our lives. When we believe that we belong, we succeed.

Works Cited

Ainsworth, M. S. (1979). Infant–mother attachment. *American Psychologist, 34*(10), 932.

Alverson, J. R. (2014). *A model of hopelessness, belongingness, engagement, and academic achievement* (Doctoral dissertation, University of Alabama Tuscaloosa).

Baumeister, R. F., & Leary, M. R. (1995). The need to belong: Desire for interpersonal attachments as a fundamental human motivation. *Psychological Bulletin, 117*(3), 497–529. doi:10.1037/0033-2909.117.3.497

Baumeister, R. F., DeWall, C. N., Ciarocco, N. J., & Twenge, J. M. (2005). Social exclusion impairs self-regulation. *Journal of Personality and Social Psychology, 88*(4), 589-604.

Bowlby, J. (2008). *Attachment.* New York, NY: Basic Books.

Bransford, J. D., Brown, A. L., & Cocking, R. R. (2000). *How people learn: Brain, mind, experience, and school.* Washington, DC: National Academy Press.

Cheryan, S., Plaut, V. C., Davies, P. G., & Steele, C. M. (2009). Ambient belonging: How stereotypical cues impact gender participation in computer science. *Journal of Personality and Social Psychology, 97*(6), 1045.

Cremin, L. A. (1957). *The republic and the school: Horace Mann and the education of free men.* New York, NY: Teachers College Press.

Deci, E. L., & Ryan, R. M. (1985). The general causality orientations scale: Self-determination in personality. *Journal of Research in Personality, 19*(2), 109–134.

Dewey, J. (2004). *Democracy and education.* Courier Corporation.

Dewey, J. (2007). *Experience and education.* New York, NY: Touchstone.

Erikson, E. H. (1993). *Childhood and society.* New York, NY: WW Norton.

Finn, J. D. (1989). Withdrawing from school. *Review of Educational Research, 59*(2), 117–142.

Freeman, T. M., Anderman, L. H., & Jensen, J. M. (2007). Sense of belonging in college freshmen at the classroom and campus levels. *Journal of Experimental Education, 75*(3), 203–220.

Gilliam, W. S., Maupin, A. N., Reyes, C. R., Accavitti, M., & Shic, F. (2016). *Do early educators' implicit biases regarding sex and race relate to behavior expectations and recommendations of preschool expulsions and suspensions?* Retrieved from Yale Child Study Center: https://medicine.yale.edu/childstudy/zigler/publications/Preschool%20Implicit%20Bias%20Policy%20Brief_final_9_26_276766_5379_v1.pdf

Good, C., Rattan, A., & Dweck, C. S. (2012). Why do women opt out? Sense of belonging and women's representation in mathematics. *Journal of Personality and Social Psychology, 102*(4), 700.

Goodenow, C. (1993). The psychological sense of school membership among adolescents: Scale development and educational correlates. *Psychology in the Schools, 30*(1), 79–90.

Gordon, G., & Crabtree, S. (2006). *Building engaged schools: Getting the most out of America's classrooms.* New York, NY: Simon and Schuster.

Greenwald, A. G., McGhee, D. E., & Schwartz, J. L. (1998). Measuring individual differences in implicit cognition: The implicit association test. *Journal of Personality and Social Psychology 74*(6), 1464.

Hausmann, L. R., Schofield, J. W., & Woods, R. L. (2007). Sense of belonging as a predictor of intentions to persist among African American and White first-year college students. *Research in Higher Education, 48*(7), 803–839.

Hurtado, S., & Carter, D. F. (1997). Effects of college transition and perceptions of the campus racial climate on Latino college students' sense of belonging. *Sociology of Education, 70*(4), 324–345.

Johnson, M. K., Crosnoe, R., & Elder, G. H., Jr. (2001). Students' attachment and academic engagement: The role of race and ethnicity. *Sociology of Education, 74*(4), 318-340.

Kohut, H. (1984). *How does analysis cure?* IL: University of Chicago Press.

Manley, M. (2016, October 26). Student: Lack of inclusion is a "campus problem." *The Northerner*, pp. 1, 4-5.

Maslow, A. H. (1954). *Motivation and personality.* New York NY: Harper & Brothers.

Newmann, F. M. (1981). Reducing student alienation in high schools: Implications of theory. *Harvard Educational Review, 51*(4), 546–564.

Newmann, F. M. (1992). *Student engagement and achievement in American secondary schools*. New York, NY: Teachers College Press.

National Commission on Excellence in Education (1983). *A nation at risk: The imperative for educational reform*. Retrieved from https://www.edreform.com/wp-content/uploads/2013/02/A_Nation_At_Risk_1983.pdf

NCLB (Act, No Child Left Behind). (2001). United States Department of Education.

Pittman, L. D., & Richmond, A. (2007). Academic and psychological functioning in late adolescence: The importance of school belonging. *Journal of Experimental Education, 75*(4), 270–290.

Riegle-Crumb, C., & King, B. (2010). Questioning a white male advantage in STEM: Examining disparities in college major by gender and race/ethnicity. *Educational Researcher, 39*(9), 656–664.

Sadler, P. M., Sonnert, G., Hazari, Z., & Tai, R. (2012). Stability and volatility of STEM career interest in high school: A gender study. *Science Education, 96*(3), 411–427.

Seligman, M. E. (2012). *Flourish: A visionary new understanding of happiness and well-being*. New York, NY: Simon and Schuster.

Seligman, M. E. P., & Csikszentmihalyi, M. (Eds.) (2000). Positive psychology: An introduction. *American Psychologist, 55*(1), 5–14.

Thomas, B. (Ed.). (1896). *Plessy v. Ferguson: A brief history with documents*. Boston, MA: Bedford/St. Martin's.

Tinto, V. (1975). Dropout from higher education: A theoretical synthesis of recent research. *Review of Educational Research, 45*(1), 89–125.

Tinto, V. (1987). *Leaving college: Rethinking the causes and cures of student attrition*. IL: University of Chicago Press.

Twenge, J. M., Baumeister, R. F., DeWall, C. N., Ciarocco, N. J., & Bartels, J. M. (2007). Social exclusion decreases prosocial behavior. *Journal of Personality and Social Psychology, 92*(1), 56.

Twenge, J. M., Baumeister, R. F., Tice, D. M., & Stucke, T. S. (2001). If you can't join them, beat them: Effects of social exclusion on aggressive behavior. *Journal of Personality and Social Psychology, 81*(6), 1058–1069.

Introduction to Chapter 3

IT PAYS TO have friends who challenge you. I would like to introduce you to Chad Tindol, who is one of the best thinkers I know and an all-around devil's advocate. I asked him to contribute to this project because his critical thinking skills are very well developed. When I inquired about how he developed these skills, he gave me a response that began to unfold into this chapter.

Tindol frames his chapter using terms like *process* and *due process* and *practice.* As scholars, these are good ideas that frame our work to become critical thinkers. Nobody in your college environment wants to tell you what to think—well, other than your roommate. For the rest of us, our role is to act as guides, to help you craft, for yourself, how to think.

The university is hoping to create life-long learners who will make the world a better place. As with learning, the development of your critical thinking will not be finished in your lifetime. This is a lofty and admirable goal for educators and for students alike. We can begin with Tindol's wisdom and then discuss how to best make his advice into something we can practice in and out of the classroom.

CHAPTER 3

Critical Thinking Skills

The Process, Due Process, and Practice

Chad Tindol

OUR FIRST MISTAKE was watching television at the dinner table. An even bigger blunder was tuning to a news channel. You know the format. Two people back into their favorite political corners and, as soon as the referee whistles, they pummel one another with labels and accusations. The opponent is the worst, an idiot, and personally responsible for the decline of civilization.

Our kids, who were in middle school at the time, asked what I thought about the argument. Rather than giving opinions, I started asking questions. Maybe I was feeling lazy, hungry, or indecisive, but it was spontaneous. Growing frustrated, my twelve-year-old dropped her fork and tossed her own accusation on the table: "Dad, you never tell us what to think about important stuff." For once in my life, I had the comeback that usually comes to me hours later: "It's not my job to tell you what to think. It's my responsibility to teach you how to think."

This story may make me sound like a wise parent, which my kids will assure you I am not. Maybe it was just my good fortune to have the right comeback. Regardless, to this day my daughter remembers that conversation as do I. In a snap, her frustration with the issue and with me evaporated. While her impatience with the world's difficult questions and issues will continue, that conversation became a game-changer for our family and particularly for me.

Despite good intentions, people who try to tell us what to think often just make us angry. We have to work through things, especially life-changing issues, on our own. The key is not for someone to tell us what to think but for us to exercise our own thinking. It is the *how*, not the *what*, that matters. My twelve-year-old daughter was learning that fact. I needed a reminder.

In this chapter, my charge is to discuss critical thinking skills as they relate to your collegiate experience: the "how to think" issue. What do universities mean when they say you will learn critical thinking skills? Is that a measurable outcome worthy of your tuition dollars? Is it worth your time?

I say yes. Learning how to think—or for you, polishing the critical thinking skills that already got you to one of the country's premier universities—is the most important skill you will practice in college and beyond.

A Real-World Example of the Distinction

Let me begin with my own story about the distinction between learning *what* to think and learning *how* to think. After earning my undergraduate degree, I enrolled in law school. Fast-forward three years to the last days of law school. Immediately after graduation, law students do something odd. I am not talking about routine odd lawyer things like torturing witnesses for fun or trying to turn your legal arguments into poems.[1] In perhaps the most unusual behavior of all, law students resume the grind by taking more law classes shortly after commencement. Moreover, these are not normal classes that meet from 9:00 a.m. to 10:15 a.m. on Tuesdays and Thursdays. Instead, for two-plus months, the recent graduates are in class more than half the day, every day, often on Saturdays too. Even more bewildering, the courses cost anywhere from $3,000 to $4,000.

For what did I and countless other law school graduates devote thousands of dollars and hundreds of hours doing? We did it for bar review, a cram course aimed at helping us pass the bar exam, which is necessary to become a lawyer. The fabled bar review course is a prerequisite for many. Three years of law school and most law graduates still do not feel ready for the basic entry exam.

These days, bar reviews are offered in person or online, but I went the route of old technology, with boxes and boxes of cassette tapes. I huddled away in my grandmother's otherwise empty house, popping in tapes like a six-year-old popping M&Ms. Looking back through the rose-colored glasses of nostalgia, it was misery. But at the end of July, as promised by the company, I was ready for the exam. I passed on my first try.

Think about this. Despite spending three years in law school studying contracts, torts, crimes, and procedure from some of our country's foremost legal minds, how prepared was I for the bar exam? Barely. I say this not to question the law school experience. Law school and the bar review serve two very different purposes. And they illustrate what colleges are talking about

1 "We thought that we would never see ... A suit to compensate a tree ... " This is a line from an actual opinion of the Michigan Court of Appeals, affirming a lower court decision that threw out a case based on a car that crashed into a tree. *Fisher v. Lowe*, 122 Mich.App. 418, 333 N.W.2d 67 (1983). It is a parody of the Joyce Kilmer poem "Trees," which many of us had to memorize around fourth grade.

when they say that they are teaching critical thinking skills. Bar review gets you ready for a test. That is all. Law school is much more than that. Law school prepares you to think.

This distinction often gets lost in education. Moreover, pointing out this distinction is, in some ways, a heresy in the days of "Race to the Top," "No Child Left Behind," and other government-mandated, high-stakes testing. Indeed, the distinction may seem even more of a heresy to your ears—the ears that have repeatedly heard praise for your ability to score in the ninety-fifth percentile or higher. The blasphemy that I share is this: passing a test is not the same as learning. It is not the same as being well educated. It is not the same thing as being smart.

Be assured, I am not questioning your skills as a scholar. Your very presence here confirms that you are. My message is that there is much more to the experience of higher education than passing another test. The bar review does only that—it helps a student with last minute practice to pass an exam. It is necessary but in the same way that it is necessary to change the oil in a car. In a matter of days, I dismissed from my mind everything I absorbed from those cassette tapes. College, or law school in my example, teaches something much richer and more intellectual than test-taking skills. Law school teaches students how to analyze, how to organize, how to persuade, and, as the old cliché goes, how to think like a lawyer. This lasts for a lifetime. The goals of your university are far more in line with the goals of a law school than the goals of bar review. Our responsibility is to help you to think like a scholar, developing and honing the critical thinking skills that will transfer to whatever career path you choose.

Defining Critical Thinking

Let's next move to a quick Google search to define *critical thinking*. Even if you are savvier with search engines than this old guy, you will not find a simple definition. There are many. Critical thinking is not easy to define. Perhaps the clearest definition to me—because I like lists —is contained in a 1941 study of the concept by Edward Glaser of Columbia University. Glaser defined critical thinking in three parts:

1. "An attitude of being disposed to consider in a thoughtful way the problems and subjects that come within the range of one's experiences,
2. knowledge of the methods of logical inquiry and reasoning, and
3. some skill in applying those methods." (xxx)

In short, critical thinking is the right attitude, applied in the right way and with regular practice. The remainder of this chapter will focus on how you can better develop each of these components to become the best critical thinker you can be.

The Right Attitude

We all have idols or patterns that define success. Professors think of themselves as Socrates, asking tough questions to guide a student's thinking. Judges want to exemplify the wisdom of a Sandra Day O'Connor or a Ruth Bader Ginsburg. Politicians want to be Honest Abe Lincoln … well, at least some do. Writers want to be Harper Lee, rockers want moves like Jagger, and explorers want to be Neil Armstrong. Whoever your hero, you have identified traits in them after which you pattern yourself, often doing so subconsciously. At various stages of my life, my heroes morphed and evolved. At six, I wanted to be Elvis, but I cannot carry a tune. When I was twelve, I wanted to dunk like Michael Jordan, but I am short and uncoordinated. When I was sixteen, I wanted to play guitar like Eric Clapton. Again, no luck. In fact, few of us attain those levels of professional accomplishment. Some people are talented in ways that the rest of us can only admire from a distance. There is only one Beyoncé, one Michael Phelps, one Springsteen. Regardless of your talents, though, you can learn the right attitude for success. Mastering that attitude is embedded in developing your critical thinking skills.

Those who knew me in high school will find it strange that I illustrate this point with a football story. My gear on the field was a tuba on my shoulder. But, a football story, particularly the story of Nick Saban's success, works well to illustrate this point. Saban fits the category of individuals whose professional accomplishments are rarely, if ever, matched. He has coached two collegiate football teams to national championships, taking one near-and-dear program to an astounding quartet of championships (and counting). He has produced Heisman winners, multiple winners of other premier awards, and scores of athletes who grab the spotlight in the NFL. Does he succeed by finding better recruits? Yes, to some degree. Does he do it by coaching more enthusiastically? There is certainly excitement on his sidelines. Does he achieve with better plays and schemes? Sometimes.

Having watched from the stands for a decade, I do not think any single factor—better athletes, better coaching, or better play calls—explains his consistent success. The common theme is something that he calls "The Process." While tomes have been written about The Process by eloquent and insightful sportswriters, of which I am not one, I see three elements in Saban's coaching strategy that also speak to your success at the university and, in particular, to the development of your critical thinking skills.

One, Saban's process involves "breaking down a difficult situation into manageable pieces" (Feloni 2015). For an athletic team, this involves approaching each play as it comes—focusing on the now, not the end-of-season playoffs. For the rest of us, this involves being present in each class, understanding the place of that class in the overall semester, and dividing the semester according to what you hope to accomplish. A good professor will have a syllabus that helps, but even with that tool in hand, you have to define your pace and your place, your personal attitude in the classroom. You have to plan because it is too much to try to get there in one day. The university has already created some of the divisions for you—semesters, credit hours, class schedules. But to be successful in thinking critically, you will have to break down each task into its core parts. You cannot wait until the night before the final exam and expect to cram a semester's worth of learning. Divide your days and weeks into manageable segments. Develop each play as it comes. Focus on the desired result, but keep your thoughts on the immediate task at hand. As Saban would say, break it down into something manageable.

Two, Saban's process, like the process of critical thinking, requires control of emotions (Feloni 2015). Notice that I did not say it requires taking emotions out of the game. By definition, football is passionate and emotional. Anyone who has watched Saban argue with an official can testify that he does not check his emotions at the gates of the stadium. Neither should you check your emotions at the doors of the classroom. Life and learning are emotional, even messy. To engage in critical thinking, the emotions cannot run you, you have to run them. There is an old saying from my childhood in south Alabama: "I'm so mad, I can't see straight." My mom has repeated it countless times, as have I. No matter how familiar that internal reaction to a stressful moment, it is not a critical or rational place to be. Critical thinking skills require something more. They call for us to manage our emotions, not be controlled by them.

Finally, the process requires being present. Saban has "found that keeping an eye on the past or future either creates anxiety or dangerous comfort" (Feloni, 2015). Last year's trophy does nothing to beat next season's first opponent. Likewise, your high school accolades—valedictorian, honor society, student body president—do little to determine your future success on campus and beyond. In fact, complacent reliance on those accomplishments may just get you beat. It certainly does nothing to defeat a competitive opponent, like life.

Leadership and change management experts talk about the concept of *presencing*, which they define as "to sense, tune in, and act from one's highest future potential—the future that depends on us to bring it into being" (Scharmer, n.d.). It sounds like a big idea, but it is actually simple. Professor Otto Scharmer of MIT expresses it in the Theory U, as in a theory shaped like the letter *U* (Scharmer n.d.). The left side of the Theory U is the path you have taken down to this point, observing and sensing the world around you. While in college, you are at the bottom of the *U*, the spot where you consider the future. The next step is to move up the right side of the *U*, into the future that you bring into existence. Theory U may just be a scientific way of telling us we must "live in the moment" to achieve success in the future. A dean once told me to "get off the treadmill," the treadmill of tests, activities, and resume accomplishments. However you describe it, whether with the philosophy of an MIT professor or the straight talk of a football coach, the message is identical. Be here while you are here.

In summary, the attitude to be successful in critical thinking requires a strategy similar to the time-tested Saban process:

1. Break it down. Break down your tasks and the ideas you confront into manageable pieces. Is the idea supported by the evidence? Is each segment of the idea supported by sound arguments? Do arguments in favor of the idea flow? Break it down. Examine it closely.
2. Hold the emotions. Emotions have a place, but they are not a substitute for reason. Be conscious of your feelings and use them for your personal advantage.
3. Be present. You only have four years in college. Enjoy them.

Years ago, I was asked to give a welcome speech to a group of students on their first day of classes. I chose to talk about a subject I knew—and still know—almost nothing about. My topic was architecture, specifically the physical separation of their campus from the nearby town. In a very concrete way, they had arrived at a place set apart in space as well as time. I echoed one of my professors from decades before who asked us to contemplate that most universities have fences around them. Universities are special places. For these students, I also described the imposing set of stairs built into the building's façade. In a real way, the students were called on to physically rise up via the steps or the ramp to reach the door each day. They were asked to climb. Finally, I pointed out the columns framing the building's entrance, architectural elements borrowed from the ancient Greeks—just like the ideas they would borrow from the scholars who came before them.[2]

The building and space where they would spend the next few years literally called on them to approach it with the right attitude. It reminded them visually and physically of ideas that would serve them well. Your university experience calls for the same commitment, the same attitude to developing critical thinking skills.

Knowledge of the Methods

The second element of our definition of critical thinking skills is "knowledge of the methods of logical inquiry and reasoning" (Walters 1994, 8). Having attended, taught, and later served as an associate dean in a graduate program, I am often asked by undergraduates, "What should my college major be in order to be admitted to XYZ graduate program?" Undergraduate students want to know the key to graduate admissions success.

Many advisors will say there is no magic major. I disagree. I believe there is a specific major that best prepares you for a life of learning and exploration. That major is reading and writing, which can be learned in any department or school on campus. It is not necessarily a degree in literature. It can be engineering, a language, a hard science, a social science, communications, pre-med, or others. Mastery of reading and writing is the secret to success in graduate school and a key component of developing critical thinking. It is mastery of a different sort of process.

A Different Type of Process

At their core, reading and writing represent a discipline of thought. It is a process, but not the type we talked about in the last section. I find it best exemplified in the ancient legal concept known as "due process" of law.

The legal concept of due process is said to date back to the Magna Carta, when restrictions were first placed on the king in 1215. Due process is the idea that the government, even the king, cannot take an individual's important possessions, such as life, liberty, or property, without following the required procedures of the law (Magna Carta 1215). At the time of the Magna

---

2 I do not think I originated this idea of learning from the school's architecture. I remember one of my own professors talking about the frequency with which colleges are surrounded by gates or fences. But, do not think me too much of a dullard. "Most innovation comes about through the recombination of existing ideas for how to make or organise things (Ridley 2015)."

Carta, the concept applied to the protections enjoyed by certain royals from actions of the king. Today it applies to any American's protections from the government, which has rules it must follow too. That basic rule—embodied in several sections of the Constitution—is a good guidestar for critical thinking, which requires a due process of logical reasoning.

The due process clause most famously appears in our Constitution in the Fifth Amendment to the Bill of Rights, which gives every citizen the right not to "be compelled in any criminal case to be a witness against" yourself, often termed the right against self-incrimination (Bill of Rights 1791). Defendants are said to be "pleading the Fifth" when they decline to testify in their own trial. Congruent with and in addition to this "right to remain silent," the Fifth Amendment provides that no one can "be deprived of life, liberty, or property, without due process of law." (Bill of Rights 1791) The Fourteenth Amendment, passed shortly after the Civil War, expanded this restriction to state governments, prohibiting "any State" from denying life, liberty or property without due process (Bill of Rights 1791). Today the courts apply the concept to all levels of government, from the Supreme Court to public school disciplinary principals.

So, what does due process mean? The Supreme Court has said that "unlike some legal rules, [it] is not a technical conception with a fixed content unrelated to time, place and circumstances" (*Cafeteria Workers v. McElroy* 1961). Instead, it must be "flexible ... as the particular situation demands" (*Morrissey v. Brewer* 1972). While that may seem like fancy judicial talk for "we know it when we see it," I would suggest there is wisdom in the uncertainty. The law recognizes there is no single due process that works in every situation. Nor is there a single element of due process required for every interaction with the government. A police officer has to respect your right to remain silent and not hold it against you—a principal at a public high school, not so much. A court has to provide you a lawyer if you cannot afford one— the city inspector who is there to tell you to get the couch off your front lawn, not so much. Due process is not a checklist of fixed requirements but rather a process of thinking about the question. That is why the concept bears an important relationship to critical thinking.

In *Mathews v. Eldridge*, the Supreme Court of the United States recognized a bare minimum of due process: "All that is necessary is that the procedures be tailored, in light of the decision to be made, to 'the capacities and circumstances of those who are to be heard,' ... to insure that they are given a meaningful opportunity to present their case."

In short, the Supreme Court views due process as a balance involving

1. Notice—being told of the accusation, that is, being given notice of the question to be decided;
2. The right to be heard—the pportunity to answer or respond to the accusation; and
3. A neutral decision-maker, which is necessary to have a meaningful opportunity. (*Mathews v. Eldridge* 1976)

In practice, due process can be as simple as the principal asking a third grader, "What do you have to say for yourself?" before assigning the child to detention. It can be as complicated as the right to a fair trial that protects someone charged with a death penalty crime: two state-paid attorneys, a judge, twelve jurors, a lengthy trial, expert witnesses, and all the logistical support the process entails.

Regardless of the circumstances, due process involves a thoughtful approach to the question that the decision-maker is confronting. It is not the answer to the question; rather, it is the way of approaching the question. The defendant must be told of the accusations, which is why the arrest warrant contains the charge and is often read as the suspect is arrested. Rules will decide the case. Evidence must be sorted and determined to be relevant. Sworn testimony from an eyewitness may be heard. Hearsay from a neighbor will not be admitted. The judge must be fair and impartial. Due process does not tell the judge what to think. It tells the judge how to think about the case before her.

Applying this same due process to the ideas you will confront and often embrace in college is the very definition of critical thinking:

1. Notice—What is the question you are confronting or taking notice of? Carefully defining the question is the first step to getting the right answer.
2. Right to be heard—What is the evidence you should consider? What are the arguments for and against a proposition? Consider all sides just as the judge and jury are required to consider all sides in a court case. Discard the evidence that does not make sense, but give fair weight to the evidence that may contradict your thoughts. In short, read the good stuff, and read it carefully.
3. Fair decision-maker—How should you decide the question? Be your own Sonia Sotomayor or John Roberts. Give college its due process. Write your conclusions carefully and fairly.

I have chosen to frame my advice around the due process of law because that is what I know best. Were I trained as a scientist, I would likely share this in the framework of the scientific method—measurement, experiments, and the testing of hypotheses. The concepts, for these purposes, are the same. They are both about approaching a question with disciplined, critical thinking.

Thinking Gray

Both due process and the scientific method in the context of your college classes look much like what one leadership expert has defined as the ability to "think gray." Thinking gray, according to Steven B. Sample, is the ability to avoid "binary thinking." In simple terms, it is the ability to avoid calling something right or wrong before you know all the facts. Sample was president at the University at Buffalo, which is the largest campus in the State University of New York system, and later president of the University of Southern California. He wrote a book geared to college presidents but with tremendous application for all business managers. In *The Contrarian's Guide to Leadership,* Sample rails against binary thinking and says a true leader must learn to think gray (Sample 2002). Without thinking gray, the leader may arrive at a conclusion prematurely, resulting in flip-flopping opinions every time new evidence is introduced. The leader will begin to agree with the latest opinion on the table. As observed by German philosopher Friedrich Nietzsche and echoed by Sample, "people tend to believe that which they sense is strongly believed by others" (Sample 2001).

Binary thinkers in Sample's world substitute others' thinking for their own. Chapter titles in his leadership book will now seem like familiar concepts to you: "Thinking Gray, and Free"; "Artful Listening"; "Experts: Saviors and Charlatans"; "You Are What You Read" … the list goes on. Are these not slightly modified ways of looking at the core concepts of due process? Are they not another way of framing a scientific method to leadership? Are they not an approach to the basics of critical thinking as applied to a college presidency? I submit they are.[3]

All are variations on the same idea. And all, I submit, are ways of thoughtfully "reading" the world around you and carefully "writing" your own next

---

3 Incidentally, Sample railed against the law in his book, calling it uncertain and unpredictable. "The relevant point for contrarian leaders is this: neither you nor your lawyers can know with any certainty what the law is today, because the law can at any time be modified retroactively by the courts" (Sample 2001, 51). This is an interesting observation for an author who also stated that "the test of a first-rate mind is the ability to hold two opposing thoughts at the same time while still retaining the ability to function" (8). Does he just misunderstand law to be a set of fixed rules as opposed to the process that we now know to be its true wisdom?

chapter. Reading and writing should be your major. Necessary elements of critical thinking, they are the roadmap to success.

The Power of Storytelling

Related to your major of reading and writing, I would also encourage you to develop your storytelling skills. Skilled storytelling is a powerful communication tool. As anyone who tries to motivate others has learned, neither a process to thinking nor a wealth of knowledge will necessarily achieve the desired outcome. All your statistics can be in a tidy order, but it generally takes more to motivate people and ultimately bring about change. How do you make people care?

Statistics are more compelling when they come with a story. Tell a twelve-year-old to learn algebra and he may tune you out. Tell the same child how he can use his allowance to get the latest smartphone, and you have his attention. That is the power of storytelling, and it is a necessary element of writing, speaking, and persuading others of important ideas. It is the way to communicate your critical thinking in a compelling, persuasive fashion to others.

Think about the great courtroom dramas in literature and film. Atticus Finch in Harper Lee's *To Kill a Mockingbird* (1982) had us standing when he passed, in recognition of the honor and truth he spoke in his defense against racism. Jake Brigance in John Grisham's *A Time to Kill* (1988) had us close our eyes and imagine ourselves in the victim's or defendant's place. Great lawyers weave a great narrative in the courtroom dramas.

When my children were young, they loved stories. My eldest loved to hear the tale of how her mother and I almost did not make it to the hospital before she was born. My younger daughter was fascinated when I would recount how her older sister brought her a balloon when she was born, and how they both sat beside their mom and cried. Their younger brother would interrupt my stories with questions, asking for more specifics about how his sisters were playing in the halls waiting on him to come into the world. As children, they loved hearing the story of their life. As adults, we continue to hunger for stories.

One of the best storytellers of all time was Sir Winston Churchill, who was the British prime minister during a period of unmatched challenge and triumph, defending his country and the world from the Nazis. In his book *The Churchill Factor: How One Man Made History*, former London mayor Boris Johnson observed how Churchill possessed many praiseworthy qualities—a gambler's spirit; practical foresight, having seen long before Pearl Harbor that US help would be needed; bravery, including "having been shot at on four continents"; and creativity, as exhibited in pushing forward the project of tanks a quarter century before they helped win World War II (Johnson 2014). But more than any of those qualities, Churchill possessed the power to tell a story —a story of the victory that had not yet happened.

In effect, Churchill was writing the story into existence as it happened. To borrow Johnson's words, Churchill "mobilised the English Language" to the cause of winning the war. Hear how Churchill perfectly summarized an early World War II victory:

> Now this is not the end. It is not even the beginning of the end. But it is, perhaps, the end of the beginning. (Johnson 2014)

Listen to how he recognized and honored the sacrifices of the pilots who flew in the Battle of Britain:

> Never in the field of human conflict was so much owed by so many to so few. (Johnson 2014)

These are magical turns of phrase. But, they are more than that. "[F]or millions of people—sophisticated and unsophisticated—he deployed his rhetorical skills to put courage in their hearts and to make them believe they could fight off a threat more deadly than any they had ever known" (Johnson 2014). Churchill told the story of the victory that was going to occur.[4]

In my classes, I ask students to write a paper on a topic of their choice. I welcome anything, as long as it relates to our syllabus, the intersection of law, and social change. Students tell the story of the legal structure that can accomplish the changes they want to see in the world: expansions or contractions of gun rights, legalization of drugs, or modification of abortion laws or prison sentences. Whatever they seek to change—and I do not care about their politics—I want them to tell the story of how the law and legal process can help effect, or perhaps disrupt, that change. Would additional legislation

---

4 "General George C. Marshall, FDR's brilliant military chief of staff during World War II (and later a member of Truman's cabinet), once argued that 'a leader in a democracy must also be an entertainer.' Marshall himself didn't seem overly entertaining, but he made a compelling point nonetheless. Even inside well-defined hierarchies such as the military, the ability of a leader to entertain his constituents is important. As Warren Bennis has observed, effective leaders manage people's attention, and that requires some degree of entertainment skill (Sample, 2002).

help, or needlessly complicate, the issue? Do courts have the ability to issue rulings that would fix the problem, or would judicial involvement make it worse? Would the change be accomplished with better regulations or with better enforcement of the rules that we already have? Would the free market work better than government? Everything is on the table.

In responding to these questions, the students marshal compelling statistics and wonderful summaries of cases and legal concepts. Every semester I am amazed at the hard evidence they produce to support, and counter, their goals and theories. The most memorable, though, are the ones that have both hard evidence and a compelling story to tell. If you want to write about guns, you can cite statistics, but also tell the story of a mother affected by guns. Did she use a pistol to protect her family from a criminal? Was a loved one shot by a perpetrator? Likewise, do not simply recount the war on drugs. Paint a portrait of a family affected. Has the war on drugs broken their family? Was a loved one addicted? Was a child hurt by an addict's crimes?

We all want to hear stories that make the statistics, statutes, and court cases meaningful. In our increasingly complicated world, the facts can become overwhelming. The stories, though. Those stick. Critical thinking requires us to follow a process of collecting and organizing our thoughts and then writing them to share with others. In effect, following that process is the definition of critical thinking. Doing so with a compelling story is the definition of great critical thinking.

Some Skill in Applying Those Methods

The final part of our definition of critical thinking skills is "some skill in applying" those methods. You came to the university with an impressive toolbox of skills and talents to master knowledge, ace tests, and explore the horizons of technology. Perhaps like Napoleon Dynamite, you even have nun-chuck skills, bow hunting skills, or computer-hacking skills. Regardless of your list, I hope you also have a talent for hard work. It will serve you well.

In his 2008 book *Outliers: The Story of Success,* Malcolm Gladwell looked at common themes among successful people ranging from Bill Gates to the Beatles. One common thread he noted has come to be known as the 10,000 Hour Rule. Borrowing from studies, Gladwell acknowledges that successful people have natural talents and inclinations. Not everyone can become a Wimbledon-worthy tennis player, no matter how hard they try. But those who truly excel, according to Gladwell, are the people who start with talent and add to it about 10,000 hours of practice (Gladwell 2008). As Gladwell explains, Bill Gates had early access to a computer when others did not. He used it for hours, nights, months, and years (Gladwell 2008). Likewise, the Beatles did not start out recording the masterpiece that is *Abbey Road*. First, they spent umpteen hours in dark and smoky German nightclubs playing covers of American bands. Their "hard day's night" work made the difference in their later success (Gladwell 2008). It was the key to developing their talents.

By contrast, Gladwell tells the story of a man with an IQ of 195. Despite speaking at six months, reading at age three, and acing his SAT while dozing off, the man never graduated college (Gladwell 2008). In the words of Gladwell, he never had the "practical intelligence," that is, the knowledge of the world, to achieve success (Gladwell 2008). Was it chance or was it his failure to follow the 10,000 hours rule?

These stories relate to critical thinking because you are here, with this chance, in this moment. What will determine your own success? It may be chance. More likely, it will be the amount of work you invest. Hard work could be the difference between being a poor guitar picker or George Harrison. It could be the difference between being a computer hobbyist or a superstar in software development. Coach Paul "Bear" Bryant said it's not the will to win that matters, it's the will to prepare to win that matters (Moore 2016). If you want to take Gladwell literally, you can devise a simple calculation of your investment in time to achieve success as a scholar. Divide 10,000 hours by eight semesters and each semester by fifteen weeks, which averages about eighty-three hours per week. Do that, and you will have succeeded in applying the skills of critical thinking.

Looking back to our last section, it is important to note that storytelling did not come easily to Winston Churchill. Boris Johnson relates a captivating tale of the time a young twenty-nine-year-old Churchill suffered a complete disaster in a speech before Parliament. Churchill was even said to have had a lisp (Johnson 2014). Despite that, Churchill worked at commanding the language. He went on to write thirty-one books. "His published speeches alone run to eighteen volumes and 8,700 pages; his memoranda and letters comprise a million documents in 2,500 boxes" (Johnson 2014). And, he did all this in the days of the manual typewriter. Remembered as a master of the language, he received the 1953 Nobel Prize for literature. Hard work paid for him. Ten thousand hours? Even at a minute per page, he beat that. You will need that same level of dedication to achieve the skills that you expect.

Conclusions

In 2005, author David Foster Wallace was asked to deliver the commencement address at Kenyon College, an event documented on YouTube. It is well worth your time to watch. Wallace used his opportunity to talk about the essential value of learning "how to think."

Focusing his remarks on the newly minted graduates in the audience, Wallace talked about how critical thinking skills will benefit them later in life—in their outlook or attitude, in humility, in learning to recognize the importance of others. He does not want the graduates to go through life "pissed and miserable every time [we] have to shop," or when they get stuck in traffic or suffer from some other minor tragedy of the day. Wallace had come to understand that the cliché of learning how to think is "actually shorthand for a much deeper, more serious idea: learning how to think really means learning how to exercise some control over how and what you think." He concluded that the "capital-*T* Truth" and the "real value of a real education ... has almost nothing to do with knowledge, and everything to do with simple awareness." One might say it is a process of developing that awareness.

The most memorable part of the speech is Wallace's fish story:

> There are these two young fish swimming along and they happen to meet an older fish swimming the other way, who nods at them and says "Morning, boys. How's the water?" And the two young fish swim on for a bit, and then eventually one of them looks over at the other and goes "What the hell is water?"

Like the fish in Wallace's story, you can wade through four years in college without fully realizing what is going on around you. You might take a few easy classes. You might earn a few easy A's.

At the end of the next four years, though, is that what you want college to be? Is that how you want life to be? Rather than being ignorant of the water, wouldn't you prefer to dive right in? The issues that you should discuss at college are frequently not easy, and the answers are almost never simple. The best that your university experience can give you is a method of addressing the wickedly complex problems of our society, not the answers. It can give you a habit of critical thinking that will last you a lifetime. If you use this time and place to hone an attitude of discipline and curiosity, to practice thinking in an orderly and open manner before arriving at conclusions, and to strengthen your work ethic, your time here will be more than well spent.

Works Cited

Bill of Rights of the United States of America (1791). Retrieved from https://www.billofrightsinstitute.org/founding-documents/bill-of-rights/

Cafeteria Workers v. McElroy, 367 U.S. 886 (1961).

Feloni, R. (2015, August 12). How Alabama coach Nick Saban used psychology to build a football dynasty. *Business Insider*. Retrieved from http://www.businessinsider.com/alabama-coach-nick-saban-process-2015-8

Gladwell, M. (2008). *Outliers: The story of success*. New York, NY: Little, Brown.

Glaser, E. M. (1941). *An experiment in the development of critical thinking*. New York, NY: Teachers College Press.

Grisham, J. (1988). *A time to kill*. Great Britain: Wynwood Press.

Johnson, B. (2014). *The Churchill factor: How one man made history*. Great Britain: Hodder & Stoughton.

Lee, H. (1982). *To kill a mockingbird*. New York, NY: Warner Books.

Magna Carta. (1215). [English translation] Retrieved from British Library website: https://www.bl.uk/magna-carta/articles/magna-carta-english-translation#

Mathews v. Eldridge, 424 U.S. 319 (1976).

Moore, T. (2016, January). Memorable coach Paul "Bear" Bryant quotes: Thoughts on winning, life, Alabama and more. *Alabama Living*. Retrieved from http://www.al.com/living/index.ssf/2016/01/memorable_coach_paul_bear_brya.html#2

Morrissey v. Brewer, 408 U.S. 471 (1972).

Ridley, M. (2015). *The evolution of everything: How ideas emerge*. New York, NY: HarperCollins.

Sample, S. B. (2002). *The contrarians guide to leadership*. San Francisco, CA: Jossey-Bass.

Scharmer, O. (n.d.). Principles and glossary of presencing. Retrieved from https://www.presencing.org/principles

Scharmer, O. (n.d.) Theory U. Retrieved from http://www.ottoscharmer.com/

Walters, K. (1994). *Re-thinking reason: New perspectives in critical thinking*. Albany, NY: SUNY Press.

Introduction to Chapter 4

I LIKE TO think of engaged scholarship as the third step in a progression model of community involvement and/or social action. The first two steps would be community service and then service learning. Engaged scholarship has the same philosophical underpinnings as the first two steps, but it involves the community partner within the pedagogy and uses the resources of the institution to improve the affected community in all ways. Engaged scholarship also lends itself to exploring issues and opportunities for research for all involved. For those reasons, the authors of this chapter give you theory, philosophy, and case studies to explore.

This chapter was certainly a collaborative approach because it mirrors the work that you will, hopefully, continue into your collegiate experience. I have worked alongside all of the contributors and watched as they have impacted each and every community they have been a part of as students, professional staff, and faculty. The case studies are particularly important as the authors have done a masterful job in highlighting pathways that you as students will be exposed to as you engage within and outside of your academic and social communities. Just like all the authors, many of you will be a part of this work as undergraduates, and you will continue to benefit from this work personally and professionally throughout your lives.

Thank you on behalf of the past, present, and future communities that you are exploring.

CHAPTER 4

Engaged Scholarship

Leslie Parkins, Davis Jackson, Jackson Knappen, Garrett Barnes, Alexandra Huechteman, Karson Holmes, Brett Austin

Community Engagement—What Is It, and Why Should You Care?

COMMUNITY ENGAGEMENT IS all the ways you can do good work in the world. This can include volunteering, advocacy, activism, or delving into the research challenges communities face. Why would this matter while you are in college? It matters a lot. If you attend a state-funded school, taxpayers in your state contribute to your education in the hopes that you will make a difference. If you attend a private university, it matters too. Universities have a mission to teach, produce knowledge, and serve the public, a mission to discover and apply learning to the pressing issues facing our world. There are so many ways that student you as a student can participate in this mission—don't let those opportunities pass you by without thinking carefully about the value of what you can learn and contribute by participating in community engagement. Plus, it's fun to be a part of something that you care about and that is bigger than yourself.

Community Engagement—What Do You Get, and What Can You Give by Doing It?

Serving others can at times lead us to focus on how service impacts communities, which is an important consideration—particularly how short-term or ill-informed service can negatively affect communities (Illich 1968; Eby 1998; Butin 2006; Mitchell 2008; Stoecker and Tryon 2009). It is also important to examine how service can transform the individual doing the service (Eby 1998; Butin 2006; Mitchell 2008). The commitment to serve in communities provides the opportunity to learn and to grow. It can provide a cycle of action, learning, and reflection that allows for learning to continuously inform and deepen throughout the period of service and beyond. This kind of engaged learning can enhance students' critical thinking skills, cultural awareness, and communication skills (Astin et al. 2000; Eyler and Giles 1999; Neururer and Rhoades 1998). This becomes most possible when reflection occurs as a means to question, examine, and critique the various aspects of service. Reflection deepens learning but can also extend service into deeper understanding and engagement as well. Considering why the act of service is needed—why inequalities persist, what action we are failing to take, and how our societal structures are set up to sustain those systems—can provide deeper meaning and clarity on what kind of service can affect real change. Tutoring children performing below grade level can provide enrichment to a child who needs the additional academic support, but what is it about our educational systems that produces inequalities consistently for students of color and students who are poor? Considering that question might lead someone to consider attending school board meetings, or advocating for funding changes or curriculum selection. Going further with our learning in our service and in our communities is key to ensuring these issues change for the better.

Fostering and sustaining relationships is key to better understanding yourself and your work with communities. Are you getting to know the people in the town or city where you live beyond the college campus? Getting to know the people where you serve or whom you serve can provide you with much-needed connections but also with teachers in your learning and service. Without going further in the learning embedded in our service, we can end up reinforcing power structures, social hierarchies, paternalism, and stereotypes (Forbes et al. 1999; Ginwright and Cammarota 2002; Mitchell 2007). Relationships and involvement in the community can also be mechanisms to better examine our own identity, privilege, and power, and how other identities are connected to different privilege and power.

Community Engagement—What Does It Look Like?

What does it look like? *Civic engagement* is an umbrella term for contributing to the public good in mutually beneficial ways. College campuses offer volunteer programs for direct service, service-learning programs for integrating service with relevant coursework, advocacy and activism opportunities to create more policy-related or systemic change, and engaged scholarship opportunities for students to partner with communities on mutually defined questions of interest. It's important to understand the offerings within your campus and community to engage in service. Preferably these are opportunities to engage in long-term or ongoing service experiences rather than one-day service commitments. Research in college student retention and success shows involvement in community-based learning experiences significantly impacts other learning and development that in turn effects positive outcomes in college. These are known as high-impact practices, and they are a smart choice for students who are seeking to be challenged and further their own abilities.

How Choosing Opportunities Might Play Out

At most colleges, first-year students are amazed at the options in front of them and sign up for lots of listserv and interest sessions to learn more about opportunities for involvement. As you start to receive the barrage of emails, think about the ones you delete right away before you read them and the ones that you seem to take a second look at. Later in your first semester or second semester, consider committing to two activities and use these as a chance go beyond your traditional coursework and to engage in something more meaningful in the world. Bonus points if you get off campus and into the larger community through these activities.

Maybe you found out about the need for volunteers in a local school. You start volunteering with kids in an afterschool program and discover this is where you find joy mid-week—and the kids you work with feel it too. The kids invite you to a school-wide event to raise money for teacher supplies and you bring friends from your residence hall, and together you help out at a booth where you run a fun game for kids and their families. Some of the friends you brought along get more information about the afterschool program and start volunteering to work with you on the same day. As you think about the fundraising event, you learn about the local school board meeting and choose to attend to learn more about the upcoming budget. Here you learn there is a shortfall, and decisions are being made to cut key resources to students, including technology support and teacher assistant positions. This pushes you to learn more about the local election and the school board candidates who support the local schools, and you make sure you update your voter registration so you can vote in the upcoming election. You consider minoring in education as you want to better understand the psychological, social, structural, and systemic factors affecting early childhood education. Now in your junior year, your continued involvement in the afterschool program made you particularly well-prepared to train other students who are beginning to volunteer. This gives you a chance to get to know the school administrators and parents better, as now you are attending more meetings and events as part of this work. Over the next summer, you line up an internship in a grant-funded program through your environmental science major to engage middle school kids in a stream-monitoring project. Along with a school representative and students, you are able to present the program at a state legislative day at the capital to draw attention to the need for more funding for science-based programs in middle grades education. Upon graduation, you highlight in interviews the skills you gained in this experience, drawing from project management, relationship building and presentation skills. Included in your references is the principal of the local middle school who can speak to your work ethic, accomplishments, and future potential. This experience gave you so much—by going beyond a weekly tutoring commitment, this service provided a means for deepening the impact of your actions, developing skills and partnerships, and furthering your understanding of the community.

Don't try to do it all. Pick those things that matter most to you and go deep with them. College has so much to offer, it can feel overwhelming, and you might feel pressure to do it all. Doing it all well is impossible, but you can choose to do a few things that are most important to you and to learn how to do those things well. Beyond your coursework, there are other opportunities and possibilities that are constantly in front of you: student organizations, leadership programs, speakers and events, sports, and the list goes on. Give yourself the chance to scan and try what speaks to you, but do so thoughtfully. Once you find the things that matter to you, build your commitments around those core things, always keeping your academics first.

How College Student Community Engagement Is a Critical Part of Our History

College students have participated in social change movements for decades (even centuries), often pushing toward or against social policies that are persisting injustices in the world. Vietnam War protesters, Freedom Riders, and Student Non-Violent Coordinating Committee members pushed against the prevailing social hierarchies of the 1960s and 1970s. In the present day, college students are represented among the Black Lives Matter activists, Standing Rock protestors, and those fighting sexual assault prevention and accountability on campuses. College students often discover and strengthen their passions, frustrations, and insights in the world. You can choose to join in this work too. You can take your education and extend it, broaden it beyond the classroom and deepen it with experience within the community.

You can make your learning matter now. You can interrogate what education means by talking about how community engagement presents different perspectives from beyond the university, how engagement offers direct contact with issues facing the world, and how engagement provides the opportunity for learning and action to work together for mutual benefit. The case studies below highlight the way in which two student leaders took advantage of their multiple opportunities to become involved in engaged scholarship. Their narratives are excellent examples of how undergraduates can take advantage of meaningful opportunities.

Nicaraguan Clinical Case Study

To many high school students, community service is seen as a resume-building adjunct to their education. For good reason, colleges and universities value community service because of the presumed dedication the applicant displays toward their surroundings. Sacrificing time to provide aid to others is indeed beneficial and admirable, but often times it receives no afterthought following the volunteer sign-out. The interactions with the population or organization in need are seldom assessed for their original purpose. This disparity is what differentiates community service from service learning. After participating in a medical service learning program and subsequent opportunities, my eye-opening experience strengthened my academic engagement and clarified my professional goals.

The program consisted of a semester-length preparatory class regarding healthcare in Nicaragua, cultural competency, and basic medical skills. On the very first day of class, I learned the foundation of the healthcare system, and truly the lack thereof. The vast majority of the population was uninsured, providers were mainly confined to the few urban parts of the country, and poverty wreaked havoc on health status. The clinic I would be working in was founded by a group of doctors associated with the university, one of whom was born in Nicaragua and initiated the clinic's establishment to combat rural and impoverished residents' lack of healthcare access.

As the class progressed, it quickly became clear that our goal was greater than just completing a service-oriented trip. The time spent in the clinic with my classmates under the guidance of my teacher cultivated my understanding of the effect and purpose of not only our work but the daily impact of the physicians and volunteer staff. Being able to discuss our daily highlights and challenges as a group allowed us to collaborate our thoughts and ultimately gave us a profound appreciation of Nicaraguan society and culture.

Even with a semester of preparation, walking in to the clinic on the first day both inspired and overwhelmed me. The room was buzzing with activity as patients' names were called and vital signs were taken. Although I had reviewed my Spanish terminology a hundred times over, I found myself forgetting simple words and phrases and having trouble understanding patients. This obstacle was expected, but humbling nonetheless. Rather than be discouraged, I was motivated to improve my Spanish proficiency. I paid close attention during patient consults and took advantage of any free time to converse freely with the patients about anything and everything. Each encounter broadened my exposure to direct patient care, Central American culture, and the process of medical diagnosis and treatment—all fundamental in my future as a health care provider. I also recognized that a key value to improving global health involves positively influencing an existing system rather than imposing my own solution. This free and reduced-cost clinic sought to remedy a small, but important, inequity within a larger entanglement of systemic poverty, unbalanced governmental power, and unequal distribution of wealth.

I decided that completing my last rotation in the clinic would not be the end of my involvement with this program. During the year following my return to the United States, I was selected as a student facilitator for the course, which involved preparing new student participants to reach their personal and academic potential throughout the program and later accompany them on their experience abroad. My position included lecturing on cultural background and prominent health problems that would be relevant to the students' developing worldview. I hosted conversation practice to help students with fluency as well as coached them through their precise clinical skills. By sharing my experience, I ensured that students memorized critical vocabulary and could successfully obtain blood pressure readings in the loudest of environments—all important skills for the work they would be doing in Nicaragua.

While helping instruct the course each week, I strived to continually improve the program. Through two main contributions, I assisted in supplementing the curriculum to fill the voids that I had exposed during my experience. Reflecting on the difficulty I had conversing with patients early on at the clinic, we restructured the course calendar to include frequent mock patient interactions. Seeking to simulate the clinical interactions before leaving the United States, we noticed a dramatic increase in confidence and efficiency while in Nicaragua. Additionally, in order to have an even more thorough understanding of Nicaraguan culture and its current political climate, we expanded the breadth of background content covered. Attending lectures regarding the political, economic, and social situations in country allowed students to be competent in current Nicaraguan society. Knowledge of ongoing societal status of Nicaragua prepared students to partake in conversation with their host families, people in the clinic, and other Nicaraguans during evening excursions. Therefore, rather than preparing students to mindlessly serve, the class prepared students to engage with the citizens in Nicaragua and learn as they serve.

By familiarizing themselves with common phrases and dialect, traditions, and typical lifestyle, interactions were more organic by nature and relationships were not restricted by language or cultural barriers. Witnessing and discussing the effect of specific political turmoil or an inflated economy on the amount of under education and homelessness largely provides connection between the probable causes of the low health status often seen in the clinic. The ability to relate to others from an uncommon background and bridge political, economic, or social factors to current disparities exemplifies the goals of service learning.

A few years after being a participant in the program myself, I took on stronger roles in the program. I felt that my college career could be more than about learning—I felt confident that my passion for analyzing and improving community health could initiate positive change. The motivation to have a greater impact began as I noted the lack of current, relevant data about Nicaraguan healthcare. We had to present the same information each year, as there was seemingly no focus on census or health statistics. Information about rural healthcare was shared only by travel guide websites. The most accurate health information was collected from the hospitals and populations of the capital city, and was not representative of rural areas like the one served by our partnering clinic. We had reliable sources to paint a picture of the community of southern Nicaragua.

In total transparency, I complained about the lack of information and did the best I could with the sources I could find. As undergraduate students. I believe we are conditioned to do this, to rely on the limited amount of information we can find in a google or database search. When we receive an unsatisfactory result, we shrug our shoulders and work with what we have. As undergraduates, we are taught to identify many problems but rarely do we seek to address them. We verbalized this issue and how helpful it would be to have research on health status in rural Nicaragua, and the honors faculty simply stated we needed to conduct it ourselves. It seemed too professional and as if our anticipatory degrees were inadequate credentials, but we realized there truly is no better way to conduct unique research than through a university. The realization that we, as scholars, have the ability to help solve the issues we identified marked my transformation from a service-learning experience to engaged scholarship.

Utilizing our program and access to distinguished research faculty as a means of progress, we developed an exploratory research project to be carried out the following year in Nicaragua. While reading through similar previous studies, we determined that a survey would be the most effective approach. For the three student facilitators involved, creating a professional research project from the ground up was an entirely new experience. We reviewed background literature, drafted a thorough survey, and had our project design approved in order to be institutionally recognized as viable research project, a process which would have been impossible without the support and guidance of professors. Additionally, we exhausted our professional network, calling upon anyone who might have an interest in or experience with a project like ours. We sought advice, input, and critique wherever we could find it. Eventually, we questioned why we were so intimidated by this process in the first place. While it was difficult and required diligence to get our project off of the ground, we had a support system of mentors encouraging us each step of the way.

The founding physicians of the clinic were so impressed with our hearts and goals for the community that they invested in our project both literally and emotionally. They encouraged us to work hard for the community, which deserved our best effort. Finally boarding the plane with our arsenal of surveys and recording equipment, all that we lacked were the interviews. During almost nine months of preparation, this moment seemed distant because of the bureaucratic odyssey to approval. Upon arrival, however, the community members quickly reminded us during their vibrant interviews of our motivation to share their stories. Each interview, some lasting up to forty-five minutes, focused on the health care and nutritional needs of the individual. The responses we received reflected the wide array of situations in the community; some people had ample access to resources while others travelled for hours in order to receive medical attention. Recording laughs, sighs, and tears, we felt that we were finally accomplishing our goal of making these voices heard.

The collection of these stories was just the beginning of our purpose for this data. In the months that followed our time in Nicaragua, we evaluated the recordings and data input for trends, themes, and connections. Looking at the interactions of many different risk factors (age, education level, income, and access to a healthy diet and health care) we were able to draw conclusions about the needs of this community as well as its advancements. Through emergent coding, we highlighted probable causes to low health status and therefore focus points for future public health programs or aid. Our data was presented to and positively received by the founding physicians and our university's honors college so much so that we were invited to continually share our personal transformations with our peers. We hope to continue this process by promoting the information we have found to help guide humanitarian relief efforts working in the area.

Ultimately, we developed as students and individuals through our service-learning experience. In the beginning of our participation as students, each part of our academic career was a separate entity represented in total by a GPA. There was no continuity that connected volunteering at a local hospital with college classes. The knowledge and experience we learned contributed to different facets of us. However, they were disjointed facets; volunteering encouraged our humanitarian efforts and classes developed our academic knowledge. This experience in its entirety, from students to researchers, served to refine the direction of our lives. Each aspect of development, execution, and analysis of our project strengthened and fortified our purpose as scholars pursuing careers in medicine. We utilized all the knowledge we had accumulated through our career not only to participate in the program but also to implement a research component that will improve Nicaraguan health. Every challenge we overcame contributed to the formation of a directed and intentional person trying to better the world.

The entire process of the Nicaraguan experience was made possible by taking advantage of opportunities. Our goal, in hindsight, was a simple one—to gain information on a largely ignored region of the world. We recorded their admirable stories and are now making them known. By sharing our information with outside organizations and engaging more students in the experience, endless doors are opened to develop this program. A life-changing experience in service learning helped us to capitalize on new opportunities and engage ourselves deeply. This experience strengthened our clarity of mission as we would soon enter the professional world of medicine with a broader worldview and intimate understanding of the challenges faced by low-income populations. Contributing to this book chapter demonstrates how the pursuit of opportunities opened other avenues to share our journey and increase the profound impact of our Nicaraguan experience.

The RC Case Study

The university setting is an incubator for developing ideas that allow students to make their own unique impact and create their own unique experience in education. From the moment students arrive on campus, they are pushed to get involved early and make an immediate impact on their university and surrounding community. These opportunities can often be found in high school as well; however, the university setting provides the optimal environment and resources for students to affect the change that they desire—whether they are building a project from the ground up or taking an existing program to new heights.

The Rocketry Challenge (TheRC) was initially founded to engage county schools, an area of the community that our university often overlooked. Developed from the notion that local grade schools lacked sufficient hands-on STEM education, our university's chapter of Students for the Exploration and Development of Space developed a community outreach program. This program involved teaching sixth-grade science class students about physics, rockets, and space exploration, culminating in assisting the students with building and launching water rockets.

With the program in its second year, reaching three county schools, all we could see was potential. However, TheRC was a typical extracurricular program with students' time and attention being divided between collegiate coursework, jobs, and personal lives. As a result, maintaining a consistent volunteer presence was a significant challenge, the curriculum for the sixth-grade classes was slightly too technical, and the launches were often chaotic. Despite all of these problems, the students and teachers involved loved the program and were rooting for its success. As we participated, we continued to ask ourselves, "What would we do differently?" and "What could this project become?"

Community outreach projects often start out strong only to fizzle away as the original volunteers graduate. Therefore, we realized that if this outreach program was going to survive, we needed to figure out a solution to the volunteer problem and develop a sustainability plan. Our goal for TheRC was to expand and reach all twelve middle schools in the county and city, but the program was lacking organization, structure, and adequate volunteers. This necessity led us to consider the possibility for the program to partner with our university's Honors College to start a service-learning course. A service-learning course would provide an incentive for volunteers to participate, the desperately needed organizational structure, and a gratifying experience for all participants.

After gaining the support of the Honors College and a particularly supportive faculty and staff, we were encouraged to develop a precursor course that would explore the challenges of developing curriculum, the philosophy of education, and our responsibility as a public university. By working with a technical advisor from the College of Engineering who had a knack for STEM outreach, we came up with a plan to pair the discussion of pedagogy and curriculum with the development of a set of materials intended to guide other programs in replicating our project anywhere in the nation. These goals became the subject of our first course, a fall leadership course offered by the Honors College.

As third-year engineering students, our liberal arts skills and philosophy minds were rusty, to say the least. We had convinced the faculty member of the Honors College who was working with us to teach a fall leadership course, and he found particular pleasure in pushing our left brain-oriented students out of their comfort zones and into the realm of social issues. This leadership course not only prepared the class to lead TheRC the following spring but also developed our understanding of the gravity of this project. The faculty member walked our class through all the fundamentals, from the mechanics of public speaking to the importance of an appropriately targeted curriculum that is well crafted to achieve many objectives. After spending several weeks on these skills, we were even able to arrange a sort of trial run of TheRC held at a local magnet school, allowing our class to practice what we had been taught and truly familiarize ourselves with the program before leading it in the following semester.

Once comfortable with our capability to execute the project, the faculty member turned his focus toward our social awareness and sense of civic responsibility. We discussed how the world is not perfect, and no pedagogical system currently in place is without flaw, which quickly led to us exploring our role in those systems. Were we necessary in the schools we were visiting, and if so, why? What do we have to share? Most importantly, if we did believe that there was some deficit, were we truly filling that void or were we missing the mark? Ultimately, these conversations culminated in the understanding that inherently by being university students we are in a position of privilege and exceptional cultural capital (Bourdieu 1977). Additionally, in the interest of improving the human condition, we then have a responsibility to share that cultural capital. We choose to do so by educating sixth graders on physics, space exploration, and dreaming about tomorrow.

Once we had our leaders trained, conscientious, and with a little experience under their belt, it was time to roll out the spring service-learning course. We advertised this course to all students in the Honors College, and we were excited to work with anyone who was interested. The idea for this course was that it would draw in a larger base to provide a steady stream of volunteers and allow us to eventually expand to more schools. Throughout the spring course, we were able to effectively execute the largest Rocketry Challenge to date, but we ended up learning and growing ourselves along the way. Not only was it beneficial to take what the leadership class had discussed into the schools and witness the reality of those discussions, but we also were able to have those discussions with the larger spring class and see them take different shapes with the contribution of new opinions and perspectives.

Although TheRC existed for two years prior, the program saw tremendous growth and success in its first year of partnering with the Honors College. We saw university students go from socially awkward, Type A students to successful presenters able to excite and captivate middle school students. The program doubled in size, reaching six schools and approximately 1,100 students for a minimum of four contact hours per student. The community took notice of our program, expected its return, and demanded its growth, with new schools reaching out to us to see if they could take part in TheRC too. The Honors College involvement and guidance was crucial and we could not be happier with the first year of this partnership. However, we were only third-year students, and this project had yet to capitalize on its full potential. We were far from done.

Despite running this considerably successful program and reaching students all over the county, we had almost no information to prove that our program had any legitimate impact in the community. We also had failed to quantify the clear development of our student leaders throughout the program, which would be crucial to demonstrate the benefits of participating in the program to the university. It quickly became apparent that research would be essential to developing the plan to collect this information, collecting the information over the course of the program, and continually improving the program in the upcoming years.

To develop and implement this research, we added an additional course to the series we had started with the Honors College. Students would enter the program as volunteers in the spring, complete a semester of leadership and curriculum development in the fall, lead the volunteers the following spring semester, and then complete a semester of research in the final fall semester. By implementing this class series, we provided a way for the volunteers to identify problems in the program each year and implement fixes the following year as leaders, much like we did when we first came upon the program. This will allow the program to continue to improve from year to year and grow with the needs of the students and community. The college students also get a benefit out of the implementation of the honors class series; by following through with our program and the entire series, the students would complete a majority of their requirements to graduate with honors at our university. This model thus provides a culminating experience for the students in the Honors College, growing from experience with pure volunteerism and developing their sense of civic responsibility, to garnering leadership experience, and finally to capitalizing on the opportunity to see issues in the world and realize their ability to affect the change they envision.

In the program's fourth year, TheRC is poised to visit all twelve county and city schools bringing sixty university students to connect with approximately 2500 sixth-grade students. Having achieved our initial vision to reach every local school, we now seek to encourage other programs to adopt our project and make it their own. By continuously developing the materials in the fall leadership course, we will be able to offer interested programs a "how-to" guide for implementing their own Rocketry Challenge, with the hopes of one day spreading across the nation. Meanwhile, the Honors College is working with various disciplines in the College of Engineering to set up parallel programs that incorporate other subjects. There may have been a dearth of space enthusiasm in local middle schools to inspire our project, but there are many other STEM projects just as needed that could be developed from the same model and that would benefit many more middle school and college students alike.

In the two short years we've worked with this program, we helped it grow from reaching under 400 students to reaching over 2500 students. We've implemented a large-scale program that hopefully will sustain itself for years to come. We've begun to implement a method to test the effectiveness and benefits of the program with respect to the sixth-grade students as well as the university students taking the courses. None of this would exist if it were not for a volunteer callout email that caught our attention. Without an interest session late one Tuesday evening, we would have never joined this program, realized its potential, and done our part in seeing it through to its potential. There are two main components to our story: you have to be ready and willing to embrace opportunities as they come and be prepared to take control of your experiences. Only at this point will you be able to affect the most change in your environment and get the most out of your involvement.

Researchers dictate that community engagement must include "hands-on participation and interaction with other individuals in order to complete the learning process" (Wurdinger 2005, 12). The term *experiential learning* is often used to describe the overall practice of service learning and community engagement. Kolb's (1984) theory of experiential learning outlines the core elements of concrete experiences, reflective observation, abstract conceptualization, and active experimentation. Godfrey, Illes, and Berry (2005) more conveniently packages this as the four R's: reality, reciprocity, reflection, and responsibility. Although originally used to describe the ways in which community engagement functions in the context of a business management education service-learning experience, the four R's encompass the crucial elements found in the student experiences in this chapter.

Reality

Godfrey, Illes, and Berry (2005) define reality as the extent to which community engagement experiences integrate theoretical material while maintaining rigorous academic standards. Often these experiences are heavily focused on either the service element or the learning element, with the other is an afterthought. This tenet prescribes a far more intentional effort in which students can clearly make connections between in-class objectives and out-of-class experiences. Secondly, reality refers to the degree to which your actions during the experience influence the world around you. Seek out opportunities to explore and unpack topics or issues that may be unfamiliar to you. Great community engagement allows you to participate in work that has serious implications for yourself and others. The Rocketry Challenge team is an incredible example of the potential of this element. University students pursuing academic studies in STEM fields used the knowledge and skills attained from their own educational experiences to make connections between theory and practice. They were able to provide an opportunity for exploratory STEM education to community children who may not have been exposed to the material in the same way if not for their initiative.

Reciprocity

The concept of reciprocity relies heavily on the previous element of reality in instances where you are participating in activities that realistically influence the lives of others. Godfrey, Illes, and Berry (2005) assert that reciprocity works as a protection for both student and community partners.

This safeguard is meant to challenge programs to produce initiatives that benefit both parties involved. The idea is that there is an exchange and that both participants learn and grow from one another. The authors highlight that reciprocity works against the more outdated client or consultant model that many engagement practices were initially founded upon. In the more traditional model, students were set up as all-knowing experts who were coming into the situation to fix what community members or clients could not fix on their own. This deficit mindset can become problematic considering the sociohistorical issues and challenges when working with people who come from backgrounds different than your own. In many cases, you will bring some privilege to the interaction, whether that is race, ethnicity, class, gender, ability status, or, most commonly, educational attainment. The dynamics of power, privilege, and oppression are key areas to pay close attention to in this element of engaging with communities. It is critical that both students and community participants understand from the beginning that the experience is intended to be an exchange. Communicating that ideal can be difficult and sometimes awkward, but deconstructing those power dynamics are crucial to making meaningful relationships. For example, take the clinical healthcare experience in Nicaragua. The student described the mutual benefit of the experience with the increased capacity that the work contributed to the organization while the student experienced an opportunity to increase language proficiency and intercultural competence. Community engagement at its best is transactional, although not necessarily always an even exchange.

Responsibility

Responsibility is considered one of the most controversial elements. More traditional scholars do not discuss the influence of social justice or social responsibility as an element to community engagement experiences. However, Godfrey, Illes, and Berry (2005) firmly emphasize the significance that this element plays in your ethical development. The authors focus on business students in their particular study and express the significance of students' continuously assessing the ethical responsibility of their decisions and actions in light of the tenuous culture of corporate America over the past few decades. Similar considerations can be made for students who go on to pursue careers in public service and policy, political leadership, or any other career or position of influence. Responsibility is the process in which you explore what it means to connect what you are doing with the expectation that you can and will have influence on the world around you with a particular focus on the "moral issues of social justice, human dignity, and individual happiness" (Godfrey, Illes, and Berry 2005, 316). This element is further defined by also exploring the extent to which individuals are responsible for serving others, with particular emphasis on serving historically oppressed and marginalized people. Responsibility is an element evident in the Rocketry Challenge experience. University students put together a community outreach initiative that has already influenced the lives of thousands of Tuscaloosa children and will continue to do so for years to come. There was no curricular requirement for student leaders to create and implement this experience; however, the students exhibited their willingness and ability to leverage relationships and garner resources to influence the lives of others.

Reflection

Reflection is positioned as one of the most influential elements of service learning, as it is the connector of all the elements described. Godfrey, Illes, and Berry (2005, 316) cite that reflection focuses on two guiding questions: "What did I learn?" and "How am I different after this experience?" These questions can take various forms depending on the type of engagement but mainly focus on pushing students to be active participants in the experience. Without taking these measures, students may have the tendency to passively participate in a service opportunity in a mechanical way, going through the motions and blankly following requirements. Reflection is a key moment for faculty and higher education professionals to facilitate development and learning for their students. For students who are typically immersed in academic content and tend to process the world around them in terms of observation, reflection can be challenging. When asked to discuss or stop and think about personal experiences or shifts in personal perceptions, many students struggle and become frustrated with the process. The conflicting concepts, feelings, information, and perceptions prevent students from being able to produce a neatly packaged response. Van Gyn et al. (2009) believe that community engagement is more than just a tool to enhance learning. Instead, they argue that these experiences should probe students to analyze their assumptions about their concept of what teaching and learning looks like. With the Nicaraguan clinical experience, reflection was more of an innovative process for the student. When you hear the word *reflection*, you might think of a group of students sitting in a circle sharing about an experience or being asked to write a paper reflecting on a particular experience. With the students who had travelled abroad, coming back and having the opportunity to share their experience with their peers, return the following year as a student leader, or contribute to this book chapter are all unique and far more engaging ways to illustrate the element of reflection.

Community engagement that addresses and includes the outlined elements provides students with opportunities to not only understand academic concepts at a higher level but also to engage with the world around them a new way. These experiences are meant to shape how students use knowledge to influence their communities through action. Ultimately, students have the opportunity to both build meaningful relationships with others and engage in purposeful inquiry. Although not all students will pursue careers that provide direct services to others, students will be better prepared to understand society and the ways that their work exists within the larger context of humanity.

Works Cited

Astin, A. W., Vogelgesang, L. J., Ikeda, E. K., & Yee, J. A. (2000). *How service learning affects students: Executive summary.* Retrieved from University of California, Higher Education Research Institute website: https://heri.ucla.edu/PDFs/HSLAS/HSLAS.PDF

Bourdieu, P. (1977). *Outline of a theory of practice* (Cambridge studies in social anthropology, 16). Cambridge, UK: Cambridge University Press.

Butin, D. (2006). The limits of service-learning in higher education. *Review of Higher Education, 29*(4), 473–498.

Eby, J. (1998). Why service-learning is bad. *Service Learning, General.* Paper 27. Retrieved from https://digitalcommons.unomaha.edu/cgi/viewcontent.cgi?article=1011&context=slceslgen

Forbes, K., Garber, L., Kensinger, L., & Slagter, J. T. (1999). Punishing pedagogy: The failings of forced volunteerism. *Women's Studies Quarterly, 7*(3-4), 158–168.

Godfrey, P., Illes, L., & Berry, G. (2005). Creating breadth in business education through service-learning. *Academy of Management Learning & Education, 4*(3), 309–323.

Mitchell, T. (2007). Critical service-learning as social justice education: A case study of the Citizen Scholars Program. *Equity & Excellence in Education, 40*(2), 101–112.

Mitchell, T. (2008). Traditional vs. critical service-learning: Engaging the literature to differentiate two models. *Michigan Journal of Community Service Learning, 14*(2), 50–65.

Neururer, J., & Rhoads, R. A. (1998). Community service: Panacea, paradox, or potentiation. *Journal of College Student Development, 39*(4), 321–330.

Stoecker, R., & Tryon, E. (2009). *The unheard voices: Community organizations and service-learning.* Philadelphia, PA: Temple University Press.

Van Gyn, G., Schuerholz-Lehr, S., Caws, C., & Preece, A. (2009). Education for world mindedness: Beyond superficial notions of internationalization. *New Directions for Teaching and Learning*, (118), 25–38.

Wurdinger, S. D. (2005). *Using experiential learning in the classroom: Practical ideas for all educators*. Lanham, MD: Scarecrow Press.

Introduction to Chapter 5

I HAVE KNOWN Charles Yeganian since we were both in college. He is my little brother in the fraternity, and we lived next door to each other in the fraternity house. We were both political science majors and spent a great deal of time discussing matters ranging from post–Cold War Europe to the possible existence of the Illuminati, as well as El Chupacabra. He is a great conversationalist and has always been a very good writer. Mr. Yeganian is a thinker, and he often puts his thoughts into words for public consumption. Technology and innovative platforms have given him the opportunity to put his thoughts in the public sphere in many different ways. I admire him greatly for doing this and recognize that it is completely different than when I make my thoughts and words public.

Charles is always insightful and comprehensive in his additions to the public discourse. I invited him to be a part of this project for very specific reasons. We should all be well prepared to participate in the public discourse of matters that effect all of us. In my opinion, this is what we should be concerning ourselves with as your faculty. No matter your major, you should be prepared to contribute to society, at the very least by participating in conversations that matter.

Please enjoy this fine example of insight written by my favorite public intellectual.

CHAPTER 5

Becoming a Public Intellectual

Charles Yeganian

AMERICA'S INTELLECTUAL INSTITUTIONS are broken.

Some of you will read that as a commentary borne very specifically out of the results of the most recent presidential election, but, in fact, I wrote that sentence in October of 2016, when I was still convinced that things would turn out differently. This institutional breakdown is something that occurred long before the election of Donald Trump, and I would feel just as confident in my hypothesis if it were Hillary Clinton who had been sworn in on the steps of the Capitol in January.

The death of the public intellectual in America, and what I consider the grave condition of intellectualism in general, has actually maintained some independence from the direction our country has taken over the last decade. In other words, for all my pessimism about our institutions, I remain optimistic that it *is* possible for good decisions to be made in the absence of good information upon which to base them.

When approaching this topic through the prism of our politics, however, one notices that the decline of our collective intellectualism runs parallel with a weakening (and in many cases, total elimination) of political norms and traditions. Experience, expertise, knowledge, and use of facts have all become less important in public life than they once were. While we still insist on seeking out a doctor when we get sick and a lawyer when in trouble and a pilot when we need to fly somewhere, we've put ourselves intellectually in the care of those who have not had to earn that station. What's worse is that we've not only lessened the impact of the intellectual in America but of intellectualism itself.

How can I be so sure? Because our national public institutions—from our elected officials, to the news media, to our financial and education sectors, to the military and police—all rely on one thing to keep them strong: our confidence. Most of these institutions rely on a pretty simple principle for maintaining their position in our society, and that is that we take their word.

When we go to get a loan, we trust that the lender has our best interests in mind. When an elected official passes a law, or a court upholds one, even the deepest cynic wants to believe they are acting in service to their country. When the news reports on something, we trust that it's not only important but true.

Unfortunately, as we saw with the 2008 economic crisis, lenders aren't always looking out for us. The examples of politicians serving an interest other than ours or the media putting other incentives ahead of informing the public are too numerous to count. As such, confidence in these institutions, and others in the public sphere, has plummeted.

Gallup has been tracking exactly this question since the 1970s, testing levels of confidence in fifteen different public institutions, and only in three cases—the military, small business, and the police—does the number of Americans expressing "a great deal" or "quite a lot" of confidence surpass 50 percent. Congress is at 7 percent (Gallup, n.d.).

Since 1979, the number of people who say they have "only some" or "very little" trust in the banks has risen from 38 percent to 72 percent as of June 2016. For newspapers, the number has risen from 53 percent in 1973 to 76 percent. Television news, first polled in 1993, has seen the number of Americans expressing "very little" trust in them *double* in the last two decades, and internet news, measured for the first time this year, splits 19 percent/69 percent. Good decisions can still be collectively made in this environment, but the degree of difficulty becomes prohibitive.

So, the question we now all need to ask ourselves—and for your generation, the impetus is even stronger—is what do we do about it? The irony of intellectual decay is that it is taking place in the midst of a technological revolution that has improved our access to information but not our ability to process it. How we use that information to improve our collective intellectualism and how that, in turn, informs our society is the key question now before you.

After a short career in politics, I embarked on an accidental career as a chef, and while on its face there isn't much that each discipline can learn from the other, I think I've discovered some parallels between the world of food and that of civic engagement. Just like our food chain has become co-opted in many ways by our societal requirements for "lots, now," the flow of information has fallen victim to similar forces. Large media companies, incentivized more toward sensationalism and driving viewership than our intellectual health, mimic foodservice corporations whose incentives do not involve our physical health.

It's no wonder, then, that our information now comes "fast-food" style, with the lengthy accumulation of layers of information on specific topics now replaced by listicles and clickbait. We no longer have to forage for information; it's there, everywhere we look, prepackaged and of questionable quality. Tina Ilsen Fox, writing of the aftermath of the 2016 election in the *Philadelphia Inquirer*, picked up on that analogy, saying "politics and policy are thick and juicy like a sirloin steak. TV rhetoric is slim and dry like a fast-food burger. Abe Lincoln wrote the Gettysburg Address. Trump starred in a reality TV show. Which is easier to digest?"

The natural pushback to the industrialization of food in our country is the farm-to-table movement. A stripping away of unnecessary bulk in order to get back to the basics—sourcing food properly, with an eye on where the raw materials come from; treating them carefully and thoughtfully; and expressing them in their simplest form for consumption. It's also an acknowledgement that some things are meant to be pondered over, and understood, and appreciated. Here is what I propose we need to do with information. The next generation of public intellectuals will follow this same formula: they will identify good, sound sources of information amidst a sea of nonsense; they will use care in how they use these ideas to inform themselves; and then they will elevate this information and share it with the world.

Having been asked to look back on my own college experience in an effort to help impart some wisdom onto those of you who are just at the beginning of your intellectual journey, I started by asking myself several questions. Most are the usual middle-aged conundrums of "what would I do differently if I could go back" or "what would have happened if I had gone to class more often?" (Seriously, as an aside—just show up. It's way more than half the battle.) What I keep coming back to, though, is somewhat deeper than that. This central question I arrive at, and have been puzzling over, not only involves how the college experience has evolved due to changes in the world, but *whether* it has evolved. The world may be moving forward, but are *we*?

It is undeniable that our society is very different now than it was when I was a freshman in college. Things that were okay thirty years ago aren't anymore. Conversely, an entirely new set of social norms has emerged, ushering attitudes and ideas that simply weren't talked about then in mainstream thought. Social issues such as marriage equality, interracial relationships, and social justice—once relegated to hushed tones over brunch—now feature prominently in popular culture. Our sitcoms, movies, and even commercials now feature the ever-changing face of our society. Individuals and entities resistant to this change, and who speak out against it or maintain the previous era's casual disdain, are finding more and more that we have moved on without them.

While this progress has been uneven, these are social changes that no election will be able to undo—primarily because it wasn't an election that brought them into existence. Instead, natural selection entered the realm of the social construct. Society didn't move forward because of our politics, it moved forward tangential to them, and, if necessary, they will continue to move forward in spite of them.

Parallel to this social change has been an equally rapid technological change. This change, and its impact on our intellectual evolution, is where the great conundrum lies. What effect is this explosion of access to information having on our society? More importantly, are these changes universally beneficial?

On its face, access to information is a good thing. But just because we have access to something doesn't mean it's good for us. In fact, oftentimes, as with food, proximity to information and its ready availability are a detriment. Your generation has much simpler means of accessing exponentially more information than my generation did. But has the information itself changed? Just because you can access all of the nation's newspapers in an instant (whereas I had to struggle with something called microfiche), has the reliability of that information changed or just the manner in which we access it? The larger issue lies in the fact that the mechanisms of information transmission are open to anyone, regardless of their level of informed thought. They didn't have Buzzfeed on microfiche. Bound tomes of tweets weren't stocked in the campus library.

For everyone using modern communication to disseminate well-vetted, expert information and opinion, there are a multitude of trolls and sock puppets, hiding behind the anonymity that the internet provides to tear down others. For every astrophysicist or political scientist or climatologist who uses social media to expose a broader audience to their discipline, there are conspiracy theorists and quacks and consultants who seek to drown out expertise by sowing doubt. America has always been an ideological flea market, but technology has hit it like a tornado, scattering ideas, intermingling areas of expertise.

As our national agenda-setters and information-distributors get torn down and rebuilt, as social media takes the place of journalism, and as our intellectual infrastructure gets reshuffled, a generation of Americans are growing up in a paradox: a nation and a world in which intellectuals and intellectualism are both dying and being mass produced for mass consumption.

It is into this environment that you are about to step. Not only is it imperative to your generation to contribute meaningfully to the marketplace of ideas, but you have the additional responsibility to rebuild that marketplace. The technological and social and intellectual advances of the last several decades are interwoven. The shrinking of the world, this access to nearly unlimited information and ideas has, to this point, been a net positive on our society (although probably not on our discourse). But there is an event horizon approaching when, once breached, the unfettered access to information and opinion will turn against us, when the internet and social media and 24/7 access to news and the proliferation of expertise will become a net negative.

To understand where things truly stand and to avoid this fate, it's important that you consider how the changes in the way we learn have negatively impacted a very important role in society: the role the intellectual plays in public life, and what must be done to revive the role and return intellectuals to their proper place.

I arrived at college as a seventeen-year-old in the fall of 1992. My prized possession at the time was my first computer, an IBM PS1. It was loaded with very little because it could hold very little—a rudimentary word processing program, a calculator, Minesweeper, and a searchable encyclopedia-type thing called Prodigy. I had a printer, too—a dot matrix monstrosity that would wake up everyone in the dorm if I waited too late to print my paper. (Show up to class, get work done early.)

The internet, at least as we know it today, didn't exist. Shadowy things happened in the computer science lab; maybe some of the more astute kids were aware of it, but not me. Email wasn't a thing either. Toward the end of my college run, both at school and at the pharmaceutical company where I did summer internships, there was something called the VAX, but my experience with that was limited to crashing the meager corporate server by not knowing I was sending read receipt requests on the one hundred messages a day I was shooting to my fellow interns. Fortunately for my social life, the closest thing we had to social media were whiteboards on our dorm room doors for people to leave messages on, although those did cause their fair share of trouble.

To do "research" for a paper, there was the library. That was about it. No Wikipedia, just the encyclopedia. If you were doing a report on, say, early political thought (like a good liberal arts student did), there was the library catalog, which you knew how to use thanks to your library science course, which was a freshman requirement. You checked out your source materials with a library card, and you tried to remember to return them.

Although my exposure to the world of academia was limited to these relatively ancient means of information acquisition, I still arrived at college full of opinions. As a student at a Catholic high school in North Carolina, we had religious-themed requirements each year that fostered classroom discussion. Throughout my junior and senior years, the topic centered on a blend of the religious and political—abortion, separation of church and state, even cross burning. It was my first experience with debate, and I loved it. In hindsight, what I loved most was thinking—*knowing*—I was right. High school classrooms are not well-known for being the types of places that deep, probing intellectual discussions take place. That's ostensibly what college is for. High school is the perfect proving ground, though, for ephemera disguised as debate. It's probably why so much online discourse sounds like something teenagers would say—snarky, dismissive, poorly thought out, and lazily argued.

While I was dipping my toes into the shallow end of the intellectual pool, as teenagers do, my opinions were being formed to an even greater extent outside of school. Greater exposure to adults and their increased comfort with discussing things in front of me caused me to pick up a truly eclectic set of beliefs, one that followed no real paradigm aside from "this is something I once heard a grown-up say." It was an almost cult-like acquisition of information—repetition leading to acceptance, which leads to that feeling of being equals with people you consider to be above you on the intellectual totem pole.

I regurgitated opinions without much thought. I wouldn't say I participated in exchanges of ideas, because that would require a depth of knowledge I simply didn't have. Upon hearing someone react to the Reginald Denny beating during the Los Angeles riots, it quickly became my opinion, too, that "I'd have kept right on driving and just told the cops I ran over some people once I was clear of the city." This sounded well thought out to me. After all, someone who society told me was an important voice—an adult—said it. I once heard an acquaintance of my mother say her favorite basketball team was doing poorly because the coach was white and the players were black, and I repeated it. I *repeated* it. It didn't matter that the person who said it wasn't a sociologist or a behaviorist or even a basketball fan. She was older, and therefore I assumed smarter, than I was. And repeating what smart people say makes you smart, right?

It was an embarrassing chapter. But worse, it was one that didn't end cleanly with the turning of the page and the beginning of my college life. For someone who was socially awkward in high school (and don't get me started on middle school), I was looking forward to the social aspect of the college experience more than the intellectual pursuits that awaited me. The pressure of making friends, of staying in the social circles within which I managed to whittle out some space, was intense. It, too, led me to regurgitate ideas as if they were my own long-held beliefs, all in the name of fitting in. Not only the aping of ideas, but mannerisms, phrases, the way I dressed—all of it was undertaken with the skill and attention to detail of someone who forged paintings for a living.

In my own defense, I was a seventeen-year-old kid who had to that point not been away from home much, not been outside my comfort zone. My parents raised me incredibly well, but arriving at college and being on my own for the first time was like jumping onto a roller coaster as it went by. Everyone seemed more mature, everyone seemed smarter than me. Instead of being the relatively big fish in the small pond of a private high school, I felt like I was suddenly very ordinary. Even when I think back to college now, in my mind's eye my friends and classmates seem bigger than me, as if they were already full-grown adults. And so, just like high school, where I sacrificed my own ideas to people I had anointed intellectual, in the beginning I did the same thing with my peers in college, much to my detriment.

It took years in the collegiate environment for me to begin to break this habit. I had to learn not only how to learn, but from whom. Rather than being a sponge for everything I heard and was presented with, I had to become a filter. I had to learn to judge the content of people's ideas, not merely their existence.

My concept up until then of who was an intellectual wasn't based on merit as much as it was based on proximity. These were the voices I was hearing. I didn't vet them, I didn't question their credentials, and—most ominously—I didn't challenge them when they said something I was viscerally troubled by. There was, unfortunately, lots of casual racism and sexism and bigotry that I was privy to but didn't confront. That I chose to subjugate my moral compass to the need for social acceptance is one of the biggest regrets of my life. The ignorance of others made *me* ignorant, as I blissfully parroted everything I heard—from actual, well thought out ideas to some truly embarrassing and incoherent ones. I thought I was coming across as intelligent, as someone who was a thinker, when in fact I had yet to form any ideas that were my own. Worse, I didn't save my mimicry for ideas; I also used it for attitudes and language that I knew didn't represent me. Even as I type this, I'm deeply embarrassed by it.

That is the power and allure of phony intellectualism, of clique and tribe and the need to belong. And this is the primary danger of an era where genuine intellectualism and cheap forgeries cloaked in acceptance are becoming more and more difficult to discern. Fortunately for me, I took an academic path that allowed me to begin to form ideas of my own. Not only did I major in a social science—a setting where debate is encouraged and participated in at a level deeper than elsewhere in academia—but the liberal arts curriculum at the university I attended put all students through their paces.

It was in the crucible of these classroom debates where my "deep thinking" was exposed as anything but. I remember being humiliated in an introductory-level class when I realized that, as a fellow student held forth on the social and political ramifications of euthanasia, I had absolutely no idea what that phrase meant. I felt like a high school football prospect who shows up for the first day of spring practice and struggles to keep up with what announcers would call the "speed of the game." High school hierarchies, it turns out, mean very little in a college environment. It was a hard lesson to learn, but I'm thankful for it. The ideas that I had prior to this process that remained afterwards were stronger. The ones that didn't pass muster were discarded, because by subjecting them to intellectual rigor, I came to realize that I couldn't defend them, because either they weren't mine after all or weren't worthy of defense.

The reason I'm sharing all of this isn't because I'm particularly proud of my story. I am decidedly not. It is instead because I'm willing to wager that there are plenty of you who perhaps have been—or are currently—in the situation I was in. It's not hindsight about how *I* used to be, but a warning to be careful of who *you* may become.

Simply by virtue of the environment in which you enter college, you have both advantages I never did and pitfalls I could not have envisioned. While you're entering your intellectual prime with massive quantities of information and unparalleled access to opinion (literally) at your fingertips, the misuse of information today is also far easier. Today's intellectual landscape is simultaneously overgrown and barren—a field of weeds that your generation must cut back if anything worthwhile is to grow.

Whereas I invented intellectuals where there were none, today they're presented to us by the dozens. Rather than public intellectuals who provide information and challenge us to fully digest it, we have coiffed TV personalities, branded and focus-grouped, presiding over panels of talking heads, each and every one of whom are sold to us as someone worth listening to. Worse, easily mimicked voices are everywhere on social media, and much of the same peer pressure and tribal grouping I felt in the dorms in the late 1990s exist online today. Fitting in is a powerful instinct, and one of the ways we do this is to sacrifice our ideas to the group. Nowhere is this easier than online, where hashtags become cliques. As with most things that are easy, though, this path of least resistance will invariably end with a bunch of people sitting around, saying the same things, always agreeing with each other.

This groupthink, the fostering of a culture of nodding, is the antithesis of what the intellectual environment of college exists for. But when discourse degenerates in the way ours has, public intellectuals—especially those outside the media who play a role in academia or business—shrink into the background. Some, like former Drake University president David Maxwell, become afraid to continue to speak out "because of the toxic—even dangerous—nature of public discourse, because we have become so antagonistic as a society, because *every* (italics mine) issue seems to get ideological labels slapped on it, even if it's not really a political issue—that they're legitimately afraid that those who disagree with them will punish the school by not sending their children or their dollars to the institution"(Maxwell 2016).

Those who do continue to speak are drowned out, destined to be nothing more than background noise in a media age where, Charles Pierce points out, truth has become "defined by how many people will attest to it, and facts are defined by those people's fervency" (Pierce 2009, 33). It is in that climate that the public intellectual dies.

The importance of the public intellectual and their role in society should by now be self-evident. In case it is not, consider a warning from former Supreme Court Justice David Souter, given in 2012 at a UNH Law School forum. Souter was holding forth on how ignorance was the enemy of, and mortal danger to, true democracy. He tells the famous story of Benjamin Franklin's proclamation that America's constitution gives us a republic only if we can keep it, and says

> You can't keep it in ignorance. I don't worry about our losing republican government in the United States because I'm afraid of a foreign invasion. I don't worry about it because I think there is going to be a coup by the military as has happened in some other places. What I worry about is that when problems are not addressed, people will not know who is responsible. And when the problems get bad enough, as they might do, for example, with another serious terrorist attack, as they might do with another

financial meltdown, some one person will come forward and say, "Give me total power and I will solve this problem." (PBS 2012)

Knowledge, the currency of the intellectual, and the civic engagement that it fosters are vital to our future as a nation. This isn't hyperbole. The 2016 election—regardless of how you feel about the outcome, your personal political ideas, who you supported, or your civic paradigm—exposed a weakness in our institutions that I'm not sure many people were aware of. The only way these institutions can be rebuilt is by rebuilding the civic knowledge Justice Souter talked about. And that rebuilding cannot happen absent intellectualism.

Once we recognize and agree upon the importance of the public intellectual in our civil life (something that is not universally accepted, by the way), the next steps on the path to rekindling the era of intellectualism become clearer.

First, we have to address where our information come from in terms of assuring ourselves not only a breadth of information but also a depth. I've already told the cautionary tale of what happens when ideas are consumed raw, but again I will stress to you the unique nature of the information era you find yourselves in. I struggle with the concept of "being open to new ideas" because that implies that all ideas are worth considering. In the aftermath of the 2016 election, a lot of ink was spilled on the idea that we need to have a greater understanding of each other, and there's some validity to that. But hand in hand with that idea is one that teaches that every piece of information holds equal value, and that, I think, is a dangerous notion.

Rather than the wholesale absorption of the worldview of others, I prefer a more nuanced version of being open to new ideas, laid out best by Barack Obama in his commencement address to Rutgers University in 2016:

> If participation means voting, and it means compromise, and organizing and advocacy, it also means listening to those who don't agree with you. I know a couple years ago, folks on this campus got upset that Condoleezza Rice was supposed to speak at a commencement. Now, I don't think it's a secret that I disagree with many of the foreign policies of Dr. Rice and the previous administration. But the notion that this community or the country would be better served by not hearing from a former Secretary of State, or shutting out what she had to say—I believe that's misguided. I don't think that's how democracy works best, when we're not even willing to listen to each other. I believe that's misguided.

Excerpts from: Barack Obama, "Remarks by the President at Commencement Address at Rutgers, the State University of New Jersey," https://obamawhitehouse.archives.gov/the-press-office/2016/05/15/remarks-president-commencement-address-rutgers-state-university-new.

If you disagree with somebody, bring them in and ask them tough questions. Hold their feet to the fire. Make them defend their positions. If somebody has got a bad or offensive idea, prove it wrong. Engage it. Debate it. Stand up for what you believe in. Don't be scared to take somebody on. Don't feel like you got to shut your ears off because you're too fragile and somebody might offend your sensibilities. Go at them if they're not making any sense. Use your logic and reason and words. And by doing so, you'll strengthen your own position, and you'll hone your arguments. And maybe you'll learn something and realize you don't know everything. And you may have a new understanding not only about what your opponents believe but maybe what you believe. Either way, you win. And more importantly, our democracy wins. (Obama 2016)

Marty Baron gave a slightly less well-known commencement address to a probably somewhat less enthused batch of graduating seniors, but the executive editor of the Washington Post (2016) sounded a similar warning: "Today we are not so much communicating as miscommunicating. Or failing to communicate. Or choosing to communicate only with those who think as we do. Or communicating in a manner that is wholly detached from reality. Too often we look only for affirmation of our own ideas rather than opening ourselves to the ideas of others" (WashPost PR 2016).

What Obama and Baron are outlining here isn't the unfiltered intake of countervailing views that I fell victim to in my youth. Instead, it is the political equivalent of a vaccine—the taking in of something not in order to make it a part of your own paradigm but to inoculate yourself from ideas not worth considering. It is only in understanding what we do *not* believe, in an awareness of the contrary argument, that we can truly inform ourselves.

It is within this idea—that a breadth of information is both important and potentially toxic to our culture—that the difficulty of your intellectual development lies. This is an important difference in a world in which it's becoming more and more difficult to distinguish "news" from "information." The true intellectuals—the ones that will lead us out of our morass—will be the ones who are able to properly vet the information they use to inform their contribution to the public dialogue.

While the importance of the public intellectual may have changed, its role hasn't. An opinion that goes unchallenged and undefended isn't an opinion worth having. That's why none of our national media pundits or prognosticators, no matter how accomplished, should be considered an intellectual. Their goal is entertaining, not informing. Jon Stewart, John

Oliver, Samantha Bee, Jimmy Kimmel, and others come far closer to claiming the mantle of "public intellectual" than Rachel Maddow, Wolf Blitzer, or Sean Hannity, mostly because they're at least self-aware. They know they're entertainers first.

Stewart addressed this directly following the 2016 election in a TimesTalk interview, stressing that satire doesn't change society—action does:

> "I think … what we're talking about is to put satire and culture in its proper place. That controlling a culture is not the same as power. And that while we were all passing around really remarkably eviscerating videos of the Tea Party—that we had all made great fun of—[they were] sitting off a highway at a Friendly's taking over a local school board. And the lesson there is, as much as I love what we did and I liked it, there is a self-satisfaction there that is unwarranted, unearned and not useful." (Lewis 2016)

When the goal of crafting your argument becomes the end of the argument, the tendency is to fall back on the unfortunate sort of rhetoric that we see infecting our discourse: denial of the facts used by the other side; retreat from opposing views to our own side's cocoon; ad hominem attacks. None of which furthers the discourse, and it is the furthering of this discourse that hones your own arguments and your own understanding to the better. There is no magic bullet. Intellectual advancement is done in the trenches, inch by inch. It's hard work, but it is also the only way forward momentum can be maintained.

This blurring of the line between entertainment and information can be seen across many different aspects of our culture. The bedrock principle of a growing share of our entertainment has become argument. It's not surprising in that context that one of the most cogent breakdowns of the 2016 election came from Steve Kerr, a basketball coach, who said, "maybe we should have seen it coming over the last ten years, when you look at society, you look at what's popular. People are getting paid millions of dollars to go on TV and scream at each other, whether it's sports or politics or entertainment. I guess it was only a matter of time before it spilled into politics" (Tsuji 2016).

This infiltration of entertainment into our intellectual and political life won't be easy to excise. In the wake of the election, the media has done a fair amount of soul searching, but lost in their self-analysis has been an important part of their failure. In their haste to cover the horserace, and to treat debates and elections like they're sporting events that need to be analyzed, they lost sight of the fact that our democracy isn't a simulation or an academic exercise. Unfortunately, the postmortems have all too often focused on why their analysis of the race was wrong and not the broader question, which in my mind is: should the media be in the business of horserace analysis at all?

Into this void in our intellectual discourse has stepped a rogue's gallery of nontraditional sources of "information." This is where the depth of the information we seek becomes important. Chief among these new sources of news, and the next edifice we need to discuss, is social media, typified by (but not limited to) Facebook.

It might seem unfair—especially in light of my condemnation of the media in general as a source of the anti-intellectual movement in America—to single out Facebook. But it's not without cause. The Pew Research Center reported in 2016, as the presidential campaign was hitting its peak, that "62% of Americans get news on social media" (Gottfried 2016). Fully "two-thirds of Facebook users"—a network that reaches "67% of US adults"—say they get news from the social network. Put these numbers together, and you reach the stunning conclusion that "44% of the general population" gets at least some of their news from Facebook (Gottfried 2016).

The number of people getting news through Facebook isn't negative in and of itself. The argument can be made that this many people seeking out information—or, more accurately, being exposed to information—is a good thing. But as I've tried to point out, not all information is created equal, and it is in this regard that Facebook makes itself an easy target for criticism. The network's "news feed" is a perfect microcosm for the overall dilution of good information and the broad-brushing of all "news" as legitimate, when, as Max Read (2016) of New York Magazine points out, it is often anything but:

> Fake news is not a problem unique to Facebook, but Facebook's enormous audience, and the mechanisms of distribution on which the site relies—i.e., the emotionally charged activity of sharing, and the show-me-more-like-this feedback loop of the news feed algorithm—makes it the only site to support a genuinely lucrative market in which shady publishers arbitrage traffic by enticing people off of Facebook and onto ad-festooned websites, using stories that are alternately made up, incorrect, exaggerated beyond all relationship to truth, or all three. ...
>
> All throughout the election, these fake stories, sometimes papered over with flimsy "parody site" disclosures somewhere in

small type, circulated throughout Facebook: The Pope endorses Trump. Hillary Clinton bought $137 million in illegal arms. The Clintons bought a $200 million house in the Maldives. Many got hundreds of thousands, if not millions, of shares, likes, and comments; enough people clicked through to the posts to generate significant profits for their creators. The valiant efforts of Snopes and other debunking organizations were insufficient; Facebook's labyrinthine sharing and privacy settings mean that fact-checks get lost in the shuffle. Often, no one would even need to click on and read the story for the headline itself to become a widely distributed talking point, repeated elsewhere online, or, sometimes, in real life. (Read 2016)

How pervasive is this problem? Buzzfeed did an analysis of the most popular news shared on Facebook during the last months of the campaign. They found that the top twenty stories from hoax news sites and hyperpartisan blogs generated 8.7 million shares, reactions, and comments on Facebook (Silverman 2016). When compared to the twenty best performing stories from reputable sites, the "fake news" generated more than half a million more impressions than the real thing (Silverman 2016).

This should drive home two important points. First, we need to do a much better job of sourcing information that we use to inform ourselves. When I worked as a chef (the rationale for the overabundance of food analogies contained in this chapter), the number one rule was to only purchase ingredients from well-sourced suppliers. Nothing would get you in trouble quicker than serving something that came from parts unknown. You do the same, providing that you're not the type of person that will eat an unidentified piece of meat you found on the ground or that's sold to you by a shady character underneath a bridge. And yet, we consume the news equivalent of that mystery meat, scanning headlines more than bylines.

This didn't happen all at once. Facebook's approach—that all news is legitimate—has been cultivated for years.

One of my favorite bits of writing on the modern media is Rolf Dobelli's 2013 article "News is Bad for You—And Giving Up Reading It Will Make You Happier" in the *Guardian*. It was the first time I'd really contemplated the idea that there was a distinction between *news* and *information,* and this is a vitally important distinction for anyone who wants to put their ideas into the marketplace, because this is the competition.

Dobelli's piece was more of a media criticism than a lament on the decline of the intellectual, but as we've seen, there's a lot of overlap in those two points of view. He even uses a food analogy to lay out his premise:

In the past few decades, the fortunate among us have recognised the hazards of living with an overabundance of food (obesity, diabetes) and have started to change our diets. But most of us do not yet understand that news is to the mind what sugar is to the body. News is easy to digest. The media feeds us small bites of trivial matter, tidbits that don't really concern our lives and don't require thinking. That's why we experience almost no saturation. Unlike reading books and long magazine articles (which require thinking), we can swallow limitless quantities of news flashes, which are bright-coloured candies for the mind. Today, we have reached the same point in relation to information that we faced 20 years ago in regard to food. We are beginning to recognise how toxic news can be. (Dobelli 2013)

Dobelli doesn't eschew the idea of acquiring information and building a base of knowledge. His problem is with the *how*. While he didn't envision the rise of Facebook news, he knew that the ill-considered opinions once shared around the water cooler, or among family at the dinner table, or even in the heady days of chain emails were now being disseminated even more easily via social media. In the time it takes to read the first paragraph of a book or journal, you can instead scroll past hundreds of tweets. It gives us all the satisfaction of learning without any of the heavy lifting involved in the actual acquisition of knowledge.

The disconnect between the idea that modern media—cable news especially—has literally unlimited time to report on current events and dive deeper into the issues that provoke them, and the shallowness with which they actually treat those issues, is stark. These cable channels, like us, have nearly unlimited access to almost unlimited expertise on any issue that they need to report on, and yet we're never offered a fifteen-minute segment on health care featuring a physician or a special report on climate change featuring a NOAA climatologist. Instead, it's always politicians, or consultants, or the executive director of a think tank who are given one five-minute segment before we're shuffled onto the next story with the most frustrating and disingenuous words in televised journalism: "We're out of time."

This setup, this theatrical way in which information is presented to us, isn't only lazy, but it's becoming detrimental not only to our collective intellect, but now, demonstrably, to the way in which we interact with each other. It shows, in very stark terms, the void left in our society by the absence of public intellectuals who are willing to devote the proper time to tackle issues by giving them diligent attention and depth.

The Pew Research Center released a survey titled Partisanship and Political Animosity in 2016 (Partisanship 2016), and one of its chief findings was that half of people who identify as Republicans or Democrats say they are afraid of the opposing party. Just less than half say they are angry, and solid majorities consider themselves frustrated. Interestingly, these feelings are stronger across the board among people who have higher levels of political engagement (measured by Pew based on voting frequency, volunteerism, and contributions.) So, while strong feelings of opposition to political *others* impacts all of us, it's stronger among people who are more plugged in.

Why could this be? Why are the most attentive not the most informed? After all, even on an issue as visceral as guns, we see instances of broad agreement across party lines, with as many as 90 percent of Republicans and Democrats agreeing on certain provisions they would like Congress to enact. Those of us who are engaged should know this, should know there's more to debates than the loudest voices, that there are still issues on which the vast swath of us are somewhere between the extremes. We form impressions of people every day that are wholly independent of what their political affiliation is, provided that's not the first question you ask upon meeting someone, so why do we assume that those who identify as something different politically are so alien?

I'd argue that the current state of our political media, and its replacement of the public intellectual, is the culprit. Chief among the reasons is the incentive that exists in the media to turn every issue into a debate, regardless of whether one exists. I've already written about how this false equivalence exposes us to ideas that shouldn't see the light of day if there were responsible barriers in place, but this is a different danger. People simply aren't exposed to partisans from the other side of the spectrum who aren't trying to make them angry or afraid or frustrated. It is good for ratings, and the media know it. This is exactly the reason why people who are more engaged feel stronger—they're more exposed to the toxin, so they are sicker than those who only get it secondhand.

By forcing us to look at every issue as if it were a middle school dance—half of us lined up on one wall, the other half on the other, and nobody dancing in the middle—they reinforce the idea of "us vs. them." To stick to the gun analogy, gun control advocates get the impression that everyone on the other side believes what Wayne LaPierre and Larry Pratt believe. After all, they hear far more from them than they do a random, sensible gun owner—even one they may know, whose voice is drowned out by the ones selected to speak on their behalf.

And because televised pro-gun advocates are culled from the shrillest and most sensational among them, those with an inclination to believe what they say are constantly fed the image of anti-gun Americans wanting to criminalize everything. Simply allowing hyperpartisans like this into the debate serves two opposing functions—it paints a warped image of how many of us agree with their viewpoint, and it elevates them to the role of spokespeople for a much larger group than those for whom they actually speak.

The way to break the cycle is to demand better from those who disseminate information, including all of you. There are plenty of ways to impart information other than phony debates where we allow foolish people speak on our behalf. Stop sharing other people's words and start sharing your own. The more we hear from people whose interest is only in speaking *their* truth, the more we'll realize that we're not as scared or angry as we think. We don't have to change our opinions, but it's obvious that the way we share them—and who we allow to assume the role of de facto purveyors of information—has to change.

To stretch the information-as-junk food metaphor a bit more, just as fast food restaurants can correctly claim that they're giving us what we want, so can media organizations claim to be merely a reflection of their consumers. Yes, the purpose of refining how we learn is so that we can stake some small claim to the legacy of the public intellectuals of the past. But today's iteration must take on an additional duty: not only does it need to reboot the role the intellectual plays in our changing world, but it also needs to show that there's an alternative to what we're presented with every day. Dobelli's insistence that we must stop allowing ourselves to conflate news and information is radical, but it doesn't go far enough. It's up to you to take the next step.

Warren Buffett once said that "what the human being is best at doing is interpreting all new information so that their prior conclusions remain intact" (Brown 2013). But when it comes to how we choose to present ourselves and our ideas to the world, the greater danger isn't the misinterpretation of that information but its weaponization. The great failing of our current dialogue is how new information is consumed not as information but as a cudgel used to score imaginary points in debates over current events. The public intellectual's role is not to riff on the twelve to fifteen stories a day that our unending media cycle tells us are important. A true intellectual knows that, in most cases, those stories are ephemeral, ultimately judged by history to be unimportant. When we boil down public discussion to this level, we miss the forest for the trees. The intellectual's role is to keep the focus on the unbroken threads that run through our society and spawn these stories.

Endless debate with the hopelessly incorrect is not the goal. As Thomas Jefferson once said, "Ridicule is the only weapon which can be used against unintelligible propositions." There are plenty of unintelligible propositions out there and plenty of opportunities to deploy your ridicule. Furthermore, being open to the ideas of others is not to say that the purpose of listening to dissenting opinions means you must change your mind. Not every issue has two sides, and even among those that do, sometimes one of those sides is patently ridiculous.

But perpetuating a dialogue *will* make you a better advocate. For you to join the ranks of our nation's shrinking roster of public intellectuals, you first have to make sure that you don't find peers everywhere you look. But once we find stories and opinions and thoughts that are worthy of consideration, we can then proceed to the second step and ask ourselves how our thoughts and ourselves measure up. Hear those opinions. Listen to those people. And then, use their arguments to make yours better.

Now, it may happen from time to time that you come to the realization that you are wrong. Take it from someone who's been in that situation a lot: that's a good thing. But oftentimes our ideas encounter a countervailing opinion and come out the other side unchanged—and stronger. Exposure to the marketplace of ideas does not necessarily mean your ideas are automatically changed. It merely means they are measured. Sometimes yours will be found wanting. But sometimes you'll find that your ideas are deeper, more meaningful, and better than even you thought.

There is a nearly unprecedented opportunity for the next generation of public intellectuals to rise to fill the void and unprecedented avenues to share knowledge. But the temptation to fall into the same habits that have bred the current generation of pundits will be strong. The current information channels reward shallow thinking with clicks and likes and faves and hearts and retweets. They turn the ability to write a hot take into expertise. They measure value in followers and name recognition. It's seductive, but it's a cop out. It's the difference between influencers and intellectuals: influencers make you *think* something; an intellectual should make you *know* something. Which brings us back to my own failings in this regard.

When I was coming into college, my instinct was to grasp for any shred of information, for any scrap of intellectualism that happened to float by. I took in information like a whale eats: just opening up and swallowing whole whatever I happened to swim past. I absorbed it all regardless of the impact it had on what my own thoughts and experiences were, and this made me almost less me. Rather than applying anything approaching intellectual rigor to these new ideas, I simply attempted to attach them to my existing paradigm. The result was not coherent thought but instead something of a Franken-stein's monster of ideas.

This method had the benefit of being, well, incredibly easy. I was in col-lege, on my own for really the first time. I had things to do, friends to make, girls to behave awkwardly around. I understood at a deeper level that my primary function was to learn, to attempt to become an intellectual, as is ostensibly the goal of all good collegians. But I had made it that far, as lots of kids do, without understanding the effort involved. I did well in school, I got good grades, scored relatively well on my SATs. Every conventional measure of intellect reinforced my belief that I was well on my way. I knew I had the opportunity at college to dive deeper, to find subjects that interested me and really sink my teeth into them, but I didn't understand the effort involved, because up until then I didn't have to exert myself mentally.

I fell into the trap of finding cheap, easy sources of information because there is a degree of actual difficulty in acquiring knowledge. Going to the library, finding the proper sources, running down the sources of *that* source … I found it exhausting compared to what I had to do up until that point. What's more, the gap between this ill-gotten information and the type required to actually be what I was pretending to be seemed huge. Freshman year was a cacophony of noise going entirely over my head. The texts were written at a level beyond the language I was familiar with. The students, especially the ones I gravitated toward, seemed better prepared. Were they having the same difficulties keeping up? Had they somehow been better pre-pared than I had? Was it that they were older? That they adjusted faster to the out-of-class rigors of college life? Or, were they just doing a really good job of not letting on that they were dealing with the same intellectual ver-tigo that I was?

This presented a new danger for me, as I now not only had a fresh batch of ideas to sift through and make my own but I had no tools at my disposal to properly use them. I elevated my peers to the same level I had adults when I was younger, for the same reason—they looked the part. They *sounded* the part. I hadn't yet realized that saying something confidently is half the battle. Those who did sounded like they had well thought-out ideas, ideas that, if I made them my own, would make *me* sound like someone who had carefully crafted his thoughts and believed them deeply. All I had to do was remember them, and say them confidently.

It's been nearly twenty-five years since I was a college freshman, and I still haven't figured out the best way to speak my own truth. But my first realization that I wasn't ready to contribute my ill-gotten knowledge was the recognition of how easily opinions collapse when they are built without care. The moment a professor or fellow student pushed me beyond my regurgitated, phony intellectual soundbite, I was lost. Anyone with even a cursory understanding of the deeper issue that lay beyond clever quips had me at sea. In college, for the first time in my life, I was asked to take the second step down a road, and I was completely unable to do so. I had operated under the impression that the intake of knowledge was a precursor to becoming someone who had important things to say. I was done listening, I was ready to talk. The fact that the two-way flow of information never stops for actual intellectuals was a rude awakening for a seventeen-year-old who thought he was ready to contribute to the dialogue.

Our opinions today are formed earlier, and more easily, but with much of the same careless disregard for a vetting process that I exhibited. This isn't because real, substantive information is hard to come by—the internet puts even the densest and most scholarly of writings at everyone's fingertips—but because they're lost in a sea of 280-character, bite-sized takes. Regardless of which ground budding intellectuals choose to stake as their own, the opportunity exists for them to consume nothing that challenges them. Information can be cultivated, collated, and easily digested at our leisure. Regardless of what idea you seek to confirm, you can find someone to confirm it. Everything from the most complicated scientific theory to the latest forwarded-email conspiracy has its niche, and there is a ready-made group of intellectual "peers" ready to welcome you with open arms, if that's the route you choose.

Alternatively, you can choose the opposite approach and consume nothing but countervailing opinion and thought, trolling the internet looking for argument for argument's sake. But I'd caution against that approach as well. If never operating outside your bubble is the equivalent of scrimmaging without ever playing a game, this method would be like never practicing at all. The size of the net you cast in search of information isn't important; it's learning not to eat everything you catch. Some ideas are tin cans regardless of how the media seeks to present everything as a war of equally valid thoughts. Blindly allowing every proposition to inform you, regardless of how unintelligible, is just as anathema to intellectualism as never venturing outside your comfort zone in the first place.

In order to succeed, the next generation of intellectuals has to be able to thread this needle: to properly determine how new information should be used. To take in new information and not automatically integrate it into their future thoughts. To hear disagreement and not automatically dismiss it as not useful. And once you, as that next generation, properly source and vet information in this way, you can begin to communicate *your* truths more effectively.

The importance of an educated populace, one that filters information, vets it, processes it, and uses it to inform its decisions, is vital. Not only to the public discourse and to the rebirth of the public intellectual, but in order for our political systems to work properly. The day after the Brexit, when 72 percent of the United Kingdom turned out and 51 percent of them voted to leave the European Union, the top Google search in the United Kingdom was "what is the EU?" (Selyukh 2016). Regardless of personal feelings about the result of the vote, this is not a sign of a healthy level of informed decision-making. There will be a tipping point where we can no longer be trusted with the responsibility of deciding for ourselves, when our ignorance makes us a danger to ourselves. It's the job of the next generation of public intellectuals to ensure that we don't get there, that we pull ourselves back from the precipice and recognize that our participation in the marketplace of ideas must be earned.

I've run out of personal anecdotes (at least that relate to this topic), so I'll leave you with a scene from one of the favorite movies of every good 1990s liberal:

In the Aaron Sorkin film *The American President*, the titular office-holder, played by Michael Douglas, is arguing with his domestic policy advisor, played by Michael J. Fox. The president's ratings are sagging, and Lewis Rothchild (Fox) is begging President Shepherd (Douglas) to do something about it:

> Rothchild: People want leadership, Mr. President, and in the absence of genuine leadership, they'll listen to anyone who steps up to the microphone. They want leadership. They're so thirsty for it they'll crawl through the desert toward a mirage, and when they discover there's no water, they'll drink the sand.
>
> Shepherd: Lewis, we've had presidents who were beloved, who couldn't find a coherent sentence with two hands and a flashlight. People don't drink the sand because they're thirsty. They drink the sand because they don't know the difference. (Sorkin 1995)

That's us. We've lost our Chomskys and Arendts and Twains and duBoises and even our Hunter S. Thompsons. Just as nature abhors a vacuum, so does our public discourse, and into the void those men and women left have stepped a new breed of charlatan. Charles P. Pierce (2009) captured this new reality brilliantly in his book *Idiot America,* observing that "America's always been a great place to be crazy. It just used to be harder to make a living that way." We've become a nation of sand drinkers, unable to tell the difference between talking-point pablum and genuine intellectualism. We conflate an algorithmically derived sidebar on our social media sites as "news," and this "news" as "information." As with many of the sins of my generation, it lies on yours to rectify this.

I don't consider myself an intellectual—publicly, privately, or even in my dreams. I'm not sure anyone sees themselves that way, because *intellectual* should not be an adjective someone should use to describe themselves. Instead, you bestow it upon people who earn it, and you make them earn it, and then you try to earn it. It's your responsibility to choose from whom you take in information, how you process it, and how it informs your choices and worldview, but then it's your ultimate responsibility to make sure that you are part of a healthy public discourse.

I'm a firm believer in the idea that things, by and large, tend to work out in the end. I try to avoid hyperbole, I'm not a fan of crying wolf. But I do think that it's fair to say that a number of issues are coming to a head, not only in our country but globally. Our ability to not only confront these issues, but to simply agree upon what the issues are, will determine the future that your generation grows up in. We need your voices. We need your generation to set the example that intellectualism is a necessary thing—a good thing. It seems like a simple idea, and, maddeningly, it is only the first step of a long journey. But just as our society has made it easy for the intellectual to be marginalized, it has also given you the tools necessary to reinvigorate its role in the public dialogue. Our intellectual institutions are broken. It's up to you to take the opportunity to rebuild.

Do better than I did. Don't mistake age or position or the confidence with which someone says something for expertise. Know where your information is coming from. Cast a wide net, but let it sink below the surface, and feel free to get rid of the tires and tin cans that you dredge up.

Use as much good, factual information as you can to hone your own opinions, expand your own intellect, and bring focus to your point of view.

And most importantly, share these opinions and your intellect with the world. There's a void out there that needs filling, and if it's not you, there's a legion of less informed, less well-intentioned charlatans who will gladly step up fill it.

You have an unprecedented opportunity to play a critical role in the intellectual future of our country and the world. Take it.

Works Cited

Brown, M. (2012, April 22). For heaven's sake, SLOW DOWN! Retrieved from https://reallearningforachange.com/tag/warren-buffett/?doing_wp_cron=1506976715.0325880050659179687500

Dobelli, R. (2013, April 12). News is bad for you—and giving up reading it will make you happier. *The Guardian*. Retrieved from https://www.theguardian.com/media/2013/apr/12/news-is-bad-rolf-dobelli

Gallup News (n.d.). Confidence in institutions [Poll]. Retrieved from https://news.gallup.com/poll/1597/confidence-institutions.aspx

Gottfried, J., & Shearer, E. (2016, May 26). *News use across social media platforms 2016*. Pew Research Center. Retrieved from http://www.journalism.org/2016/05/26/news-use-across-social-media-platforms-2016/

Lewis, H. (2016, December). Jon Stewart talks media's role in election outcome, how to combat spread of fake news. *The Hollywood Reporter*. Retrieved from http://www.hollywoodreporter.com/news/jon-stewart-why-daily-show-didnt-determine-election-trump-fake-news-cnn-fox-at-ny-times-talk-95

Maxwell, D. (2016, July). Where have all the voices gone. *Huffington Post*. Retrieved from http://www.huffingtonpost.com/entry/where-have-all-the-voices-gone_us_5792379be4b0a1917a6e7c8f

Obama, B. (2016, May). *Remarks by the president at commencement address at Rutgers, the state university of New Jersey*. Office of the Press Secretary, the White House. Retrieved from https://obamawhitehouse.archives.gov/the-press-office/2016/05/15/remarks-president-commencement-address-rutgers-state-university-new

Partisanship and political animosity in 2016. (2016, June). Pew Research Center. Retrieved from http://www.people-press.org/2016/06/22/partisanship-and-political-animosity-in-2016/

PBS NewsHour (Producer). (2012). Former Supreme Court Justice Souter on the danger of America's "pervasive civic ignorance." Available from https://www.youtube.com/watch?v=rWcVtWennr0

Pierce, C. (2009) *Idiot America: How stupidity became a virtue in the land of the free.* New York, NY: Doubleday.

Read, M. (2016, November 9). Donald Trump won because of Facebook. *New York Magazine*. Retrieved from http://nymag.com/selectall/2016/11/donald-trump-won-because-of-facebook.html

Selyukh, A. 2016. (2016, June 24). After Brexit vote, Britain asks Google: "What is the EU?" *National Public Radio*. Retrieved from http://www.npr.org/sections/alltechconsidered/2016/06/24/480949383/britains-google-searches-for-what-is-the-eu-spike-after-brexit-vote

Silverman, C. (2016, November 16). This analysis shows how viral fake election news stories outperformed real news on Facebook. *Buzzfeed*. Retrieved from https://www.buzzfeed.com/craigsilverman/

viral-fake-election-news-outperformed-real-news-on-facebook?utm_term=.owQM-rDlpE#.gmqA0PqlY

Sorkin, A. (Producer), & Reiner, R. (Director). (1995). *The American President* [Motion Picture]. United States: Castle Rock Entertainment.

Tsuji, A. (2016, November 9). Steve Kerr goes on pregame rant about presidential election: "I thought we were better than this." *USA Today*. Retrieved from http://ftw.usato-day.com/2016/11/warriors-steve-kerr-trump-presidential-election-rant-america

WashPost PR. (2016, May 6). Martin Baron addresses Temple University graduates [Web log post]. Retrieved from https://www.washingtonpost.com/pr/wp/2016/05/06/martin-baron-adresses-temple-university-graduates/?utm_term=.5aefc145032f

Introduction to Chapter 6

ONE OF THE things you will be asked to do in your career is to write a personal statement. You have already done this several times in your scholarly pursuits. You told some admissions counselor why you wanted to be a part of your current academic community. You typed out a generalized statement of who you are (identity) and what you plan to make of this wonderful opportunity to become enlightened (agency). There is a skill to constructing this narrative; it is important to be able to clearly articulate your story as an individual and as a scholar.

I have worked with Dr. Alexandra Gonzenbach Perkins in and out of the classroom, and I think she frames the need for narrative very nicely. Her contribution to this work is important because you are not done constructing your own narrative; in fact, you are in many ways at the beginning of deciding who you are and what you will do. One of the reasons I like working with college students so much is that we get to see your past, present, and future selves in the time we are together. It is an interesting mix of narratives, and helping you construct your narratives is one of the most important things we can do as faculty, staff, and administrators.

It is my hope that you will use the language of narrative, identity, and agency going forward. It is very helpful as you begin to construct your personal and professional self.

CHAPTER 6

Developing Identity and Agency as a Scholar

Alexandra Gonzenbach Perkins

An Introduction

WE TELL STORIES every day. Not in the deeply Southern sense of the word, which evokes the telling of lies, fibs, or tall tales, but rather in the sense that, every day, we shape our experiences, views, and feelings through language. Language refers to anything that communicates our ideas to others around us. These can be the conversations we have with our friends, the essays we write for our courses, or even the photos we share on social media. Each of these stories communicates information to a larger audience but also demonstrates the generative power of language. Language is a tool that helps us understand and share our world. It is the medium we use to position ourselves as subjects. The discourses we create are not merely given; they are always produced by a subject. We utilize language to shape who we are and communicate that sense of self to others. It is through language that we develop identity and agency. This is the central thesis of this chapter. We will explore how we utilize narrative to create agency and identity as scholars.

Within the context of your university community, students will develop agency and identity as scholars. You will push yourself to understand new and challenging viewpoints, you will position yourself within various debates, and you will begin to share your unique perspective as a scholar. In your scholarly creation, be it literary essays, artistic works, or data analyses, you will leave an indelible trace upon the already vast fields of knowledge housed both within and without academia. While many of the examples in this chapter come from my personal experience in literary and cultural studies, the central argument of this chapter is applicable, and indeed essential, to all areas of study. Whether you major in math, theater, or public relations, developing a scholarly voice allows you to put your own mark on your field of academic inquiry. In this journey, it is prescient to understand the role that narrative plays in developing a scholarly identity. This chapter reflects upon narrative as a central tool for creating identity and agency as both a scholar and as a human being. Again, narrative is part of our everyday lives, yet it is not something we reflect upon regularly. This chapter considers what happens when we become aware of the role narrative plays in our lives and in the relationships we develop with others. As we develop an awareness of the ubiquity of narrative in our lives, we begin to understand the impact it has for our ever-evolving sense of self as well as the impact our identity has upon the world around us, both globally and locally.

What Is Narrative?

Narrative has a deceptively simple definition: a story that is written or told. Within the beautiful simplicity of this definition, however, we find a number of important implications. First, we must consider types of narrative genres. If a narrative is a story that is written or told, *how* can this story be written or told? Most university students will think immediately of novels or films. Indeed, these are genres that we use to study various narrative conventions, such as plot, characters, and point of view. However, nearly every communicative gesture develops a narrative. Consider, for example, an argumentative essay written for a freshman composition course. Your position on a topic, the data you use to support your conclusions, and the way in which you structure your arguments form a story—a narrative—of your ideas. What about visual narratives? We have already mentioned films, which incorporate dialogue and visual elements. Can a narrative exist without words? Most certainly. Take a moment to study the following image:

Velázquez, Diego. *Las Meninas or The Family of Philip IV 1656–1657.* Oil on Canvas, Museo del Prado, Madrid.

Source: https://commons.wikimedia.org/wiki/File:Diego_Vel%C3%A1zquez_Las_Meninas_Die_Hof-fr%C3%A4ulein.jpg.

Who is the focus of this painting? What is the subject of this painting? If we look carefully, the artist himself, Diego Velázquez, is featured to the left of the central figure in the painting, the Infanta Margarita, daughter of the Spanish King Philip IV and Queen Mariana. We also notice that the artist is standing in front of a canvas. If the subject of this painting is the little girl in the white dress at the center of the painting, how can the artist possibly be painting her, if he is standing behind her? The artist, in fact, is facing the viewer. Could he be painting us? While tempting, this is quite unlikely. Look at the back wall represented in the painting. You will notice a number of paintings on the wall, yet one stands out more brightly than the others. Is this really a painting? Closer inspection reveals that this is actually a mirror, reflecting the figures of King Philip and Queen Mariana.

While the subject of the painting we are viewing is the Infanta Margarita and her entourage of ladies-in-waiting, the subject of the painting within the painting (the canvas we see Velázquez painting) is the king and queen of Spain. Velázquez constructs a visual narrative that tells various stories. Not only does he represent important figures in the Spanish court of the Golden Age, he also constructs a meta-narrative about representation itself. The way in which he positions himself in the narrative frame of the canvas, as well as how he paints the king and queen while guiding the viewer to focus upon the Infanta Margarita, demonstrates Velazquez's skillful use of narrative to comment upon the practice of representation in painting.

In Velázquez's work, the viewer must confront their own position as a viewer in relationship to the genre of painting. For a more contemporary example, think about how we use images to tell the story of our daily lives on social media apps such as Instagram or Snapchat. While we may include brief comments about the images, the images themselves tell a story. Narrative shapes our daily lives in many ways. It helps us understand our position in the world, while serving as a tool that we use to share our position in the world. More importantly, narrative is one way that we shape our own world. Here we can see the connections narrative has to identity and agency. We become the authors of our own worlds. We are creators, and the world is our canvas. Identity and agency are shaped by and help shape our positions in the world. How do we define complex concepts such as identity and agency? For the purpose of this chapter, which considers the relationship between narrative, identity, and agency, I use *identity* as a term to describe the chosen and given social categories that we use to differentiate ourselves from and to assimilate ourselves to others. *Agency* refers to our ability to act in any given situation. This is merely a starting point for these definitions. Throughout the chapter we will develop more nuanced definitions of all these concepts, especially as we analyze the relationships among the three.

Why Is Narrative Important?

Perhaps as a child (or even recently) you heard the old refrain "sticks and stones may break my bones but words can never hurt me." Paradoxically, this is a phrase we tend to hear when words have indeed hurt us. Words are powerful tools. Not only do words help us communicate with others, but the words we use convey a lot about ourselves. The slang we use marks us generationally; regional vocabulary tells people where we are from; and our accents can reveal a number of things about us, from our country of birth to our native languages. These are elements of language seemingly out of our control. Yet we do have power over language, what it communicates about us, and how we use it to communicate with others.

Consider, for example, the recent proliferation of linguistic markers we use to describe gender. The English language provides us with two articulations of gendered pronouns: masculine and feminine. For some, however, this binary structure of gendered language does not reflect the reality of their lived experience. For this reason, we have developed options that lie outside of this binary, from the relatively gender neutral they/them/theirs, to neologisms such as xe/xem/xir. As we will see, language is never innocent nor is it purely descriptive. While we use language to describe our world, language also has the power to produce and reproduce certain realities. Let us look at two sentences to understand the productive power of language.

The class has twenty students.

This sentence is pretty straightforward. It describes an observable reality and communicates concrete information. Now, let us take a look at a different kind of sentence.

I nominate Rebecca for class president.

This sentence presents a different communicative function than mere description. The sentence itself performs the action that it describes. This type of sentence or utterance is what J. L. Austin (1975) calls a performative. With these types of utterances, we not only say something, we do something as well. The statement is not merely descriptive; it enacts the action that it describes. Theorists such as Judith Butler (1993) have taken the idea of performative speech acts and attached them to different categories of identity, such as gender. In doing so, we begin to see how language not only describes certain realities but creates and enforces realities that we tend to take for granted. That is, we understand these realities as given or imposed rather than socially constructed and upheld through reiteration. As an example, we can consider Butler's work on gender as a social construct. For Butler, gender identities are not innate, they are not identities we are born with. Rather, they are identities that are constantly produced, enforced, and reiterated through language and action in a given society. While a rather simple example, the fact that we associate our gender binary with the colors pink and blue is neither natural nor given. It is a characteristic that Western society, particularly in the United States, has chosen, produced, and reinforced.

Herein lies the power of narrative. If the language we use goes beyond description, we have in our hands a powerful tool for creation. As for identity and agency, narrative is a principal way that we make sense of our world, communicate that understanding to others, and create communities around this understanding. Narrative is also tied to questions of identity and identification. We use narrative to communicate who we are as individuals *and* to create community upon the basis of how we identify ourselves. Our narratives are acts of agency. We create and claim spaces for ourselves. Creating narratives can be challenging due to the fact that narrative in itself presents certain tensions. However, in agreement with Michael Bamberg, "navigating and connecting temporal continuity and discontinuity, self and other differentiation, and the direction of fit between person and world, take place in the small stories told on everyday occasions in which tellers affirm a sense of who they are" (Bamberg 2009, 134).

As a Student, What Is Your Relationship to Narrative?

As we have explored, narrative is a powerful tool for creating and sharing your place in the world. Beyond your personal experiences, you will experience the narratives of others. Narrative is a key element in communication between yourself, your peers, and your professors. Beyond the personal level of narratives of the people you meet, you will also be exposed to a variety of narratives in the classroom. Contact with the academic level of narrative will help you to shape your own narrative. Through narrative, we can experience the lives of others, whether through seventeenth-century Spanish novels, twenty-first-century Latin American film, or statistical analyses of population density in twentieth-century China. Again, narrative appears in all fields of study. We create narrative to share experiences, interpret data, and analyze statistics. As a student, you will be exposed to a variety of narratives that will shape your interpretation of the world. It is important to recognize and embrace the fact that you, as a student and as a human being, are always growing, changing, and evolving. It is narrative that helps us make sense of our ever-evolving selves.

What Is the Relationship between Narrative and Identity?

Let us take a moment to consider the elements that make a person who they are. What makes you a subject in the world? The notion of "self," that elusive marker of who we are, the concept that we construct in relation to others, experiences a dynamic shift in the late twentieth century. Before the emergence of postmodernism in the mid-seventies and early eighties, the self was understood as autonomous and given. That is to say, the self was a fixed entity. With the development of postmodern theories of social institutions and their impact on subjects, we begin to understand the self as a subjective experience rather than a given identity. The postmodern self acknowledges the fragmentary nature of identity as well as the influence that various social structures (school, law, religion, family, etc.) have upon the constitution of the self. Following Harlene Anderson, the postmodern understanding of self stems from "a shift from a modernist logical understanding (verifiable reality) of self to a narrative social understanding (constructed reality) of self" (2008, 211–12). Narrative is a central element to understanding both subjectivity (i.e., the position of the self in the world) and identity.

Narrative is not without its critiques and challenges. Catriona Mackenzie highlights some of the critiques that emerge when we use narrative to understand our position in the world. Narrative, as explored previously, is the ordering of events into a coherent, forward-moving story line. However, the coherence we create when telling the story of our lives does not always reflect lived experience. Our lives are not straightforward, linear accounts. A further critique highlighted by Mackenzie is that the narrative constructions of our lives leave out or ignore randomness and contingency that is part of our daily lives (2009, 106). Our lives are composed of random events, feelings, and interactions that are typically neither linear nor cohesive. For example, when I tell someone about my day, I select the most important events and relay them in a chronological, orderly manner. I probably would not include the random thoughts that punctuate my day, the various casual interactions with friends and colleagues, or the unimpressive snacks I consume throughout the day. However, these are all parts of my lived experience.

Narrative provides unique ways of piecing together the variety of experiences that make up our lives. A strength of narrative, following Mackenzie, is "that the different episodes and happenings and the relations among the characters are meaningful by virtue of the role they play in the overall narrative sequence. Narrative is an organizing principle or a structure for interpreting the events and characters that makes sense of what happens, and makes the sayings and doings of the characters intelligible" (106-7). This is central to our analysis of the importance of narrative. Narrative structures how we understand our world. That I select to tell the important elements of my day demonstrates Mackenzie's quote. Beyond being an organizing principle for the self, we must consider the active role that narrative affords to the subject. Other academics have described the importance of narrative as an organizing principle of our lives. Following Anderson, "narrative is a dynamic process that constitutes both the way we organize the events and experiences of our lives to make sense of them and the way we participate in creating the things we make sense of, including ourselves" (212). Significantly, the narratives we create are not merely descriptive; they shape and reshape the world around us.

The narratives we create go beyond painting a picture of how we understand the world. To follow the metaphor, the pictures we create influence how others see our world, which in turn shapes their experiences of the world. Think of a time you saw an image that really impacted you. Perhaps it is a photograph or a painting you can never forget, whether for its positive or negative impact. This image, this narrative telling of how one person experiences the world, has now influenced your story. It may not fundamentally change how you view the world, but in some small way it has changed you.

Our lives shape and are shaped by narrative. Owing to this postmodern turn in how we understand the self and its relationship to the world, we now understand that the self, who we are, is a dynamic process, rather than a static being. The self, as we describe it through narrative, is never a totalizing nor totalized entity. It is a self that is always in process and always changing within the realm of language. As eloquently stated by Anderson, "self, therefore, is always engaged in conversational becoming" (216). However, if the self is always becoming, and never really "is" in the present moment, how do we begin to talk about identity and agency? If we understand identity as those various categories that make us who we are and agency as what we can do, how do we engage these two ideas in a process that is always shifting and ongoing? We must consider the relationship between narrative and agency.

What Is the Relationship between Narrative and Agency?

Let us begin with another quote from Anderson: "In a postmodern view the problem of *identity* and *continuity* or what we think of as our *selfhood* becomes maintaining coherence and continuity in the stories we tell about ourselves" (217; emphasis in original). We strive for unified identities. We consistently work to present ourselves as a specific person in a given context.

However, we must acknowledge that the self is in constant development. Typically, however, we describe ourselves as unified beings, despite the constant changes undergone by both our bodies and our minds.

As previously described, the tension between temporal continuity and discontinuity is a challenge we face when using narrative to frame our lives and experiences. We have to consider the mutual existence of change and continuity within the subject. Think about a time that you had a really terrible day, week, or even month. Perhaps you described yourself during this time as "not being like yourself," and perhaps upon the resolution of this terrible time, people state they are "happy to have the old you back." These statements present a problematic understanding of the self, an understanding that posits the self as divisible among different temperaments. Even during that difficult time, you were still you. A version of yourself emerged, perhaps a version before unseen, yet it was not a wholly separate entity.

The movement back and forth between various subject positions that constructs our notion of self is central to understanding the power narrative has for shaping our self, identity, and agency. There may be multiple iterations of our concept of self. Naturally, we act differently in various contexts. How you speak and interact with a close friend is different from how you talk to a professor in class. However, all of these iterations are *you*. Following Hermans et al., "the multiplicity of the self does not result in fragmentation, because it is the same I that is moving back and forth between several positions" (cited in Anderson, 221). As for the question of agency, we must consider again the role that we, as co-creators of our own narratives, play in the formation of new possibilities in the world. We are agentic beings in the mere construction of narratives. We make things happen. Furthermore, narratives provide to us a sense of self. However, perhaps the strongest link between agency and narrative develops from "participating in the creation of the expansion of possible choices" (Anderson 2008, 231). Narrative exists in a space of creative tension. Narrative is a tool that we use to understand our world, while it simultaneously shapes us and our understanding of our world.

This tension is augmented by the fact that we are never the sole authors of our narratives. Various people and situations in our lives shape who we are as well. Identity, while autonomous and personal, is always co-constructed. We depend upon others for recognition, and in this recognition, we form our position as subjects in the world, our identities. To underscore the importance of recognition in the formation of the self, consider the following scenario. You walk into an ice cream shop and no one acknowledges you. You consider this unpleasant interaction a case of poor customer service and move on. Next, when you leave the shop, no one seems to see you. You hold the door for a person on the way out, and they do not acknowledge your gesture. You may consider them rude, unfriendly, or perhaps just busy. As you continue through your day, not a single person responds to you or otherwise acknowledges your existence. Imagine this going on for days or weeks. At a certain point, you may begin to question your existence. Why? Because, as human beings, we depend upon recognition to assure our own existence. We develop a reciprocal relationship with the other, be it a friend or a stranger, to situate ourselves in the world as subjects. This relationship is tied to our construction and conceptualization of self. If we rely upon the other for our own self-actualization, certainly this influence will appear, even in small ways, in the narratives we construct. For if narrative is the way we make sense of our world as well as the vehicle we use to share this perspective with the world, then our narratives are necessarily dependent upon recognition and some form of mutual understanding. We are the authors of our own selves.

We are never, however, the sole authors of our own identities. Many factors shape who we are and how we express that identity. Following Holland et al. (2001), the "I" is built with preexisting materials: "the 'I' draws upon the languages, the dialects, the worlds of others to which she has been exposed" (170). Furthermore, the self, understood as our identity, exists in a space of becoming rather than as a thing that exists statically in the world. In agreement with Holland et al., "because the self is the nexus of a continuing flow of activity and is participating in this activity, it cannot be finalized" (173). That is to say, we are never the same person in any given moment in time, as our experiences mold and change who we are. It is rare that we change radically from day to day or minute to minute. The changes we experience are usually slow and sustained, evolving over the course of time. There are events, however, that dramatically shift our understanding of ourselves and our place in the world. Whether large or small, these shifts in our self-conceptualization fit within a consideration of narrative, as the story always continues.

How Do Agency, Identity, and Narrative Work Together?

We find simple yet profound definition of identity in the words of philosopher Christine Korsgaard, who sees identity as "a role with a point" (2009, 21). This definition leads us to the fundamental role of identity, which is action. Identity comes from various sources. There are identities that we adopt and identities that are imposed upon us. There are identities we can control and others we cannot. However, our identities, be they chosen or conferred, are always shaped by the actions we take. Following Korsgaard, "it is in choosing your actions you create that identity. What this means is that you constitute yourself *as* the author of your actions in the very act of choosing them" (20; emphasis in original). Notably, Korsgaard uses the word "author" in her explanation of the relationship between action and identity. This brings us again to the intersection of narrative, identity, and agency. If action is self-constitution, the creation of the self and of identity, then action is necessarily a narrative function of the way in which we shape our identities. Therefore, we can see quite clearly the direct relationship between agency and identity, as well as the role of narrative in shaping both.

Narrative is everywhere. Mieke Bal (2009) highlights the ubiquity of narrative, stating "narratology [the study of narrative] applies to virtually every cultural object. Not that everything 'is' narrative; but practically everything in culture has a narrative aspect to it, or at the very least, can be perceived, interpreted as narrative" (225). Narrative permeates our understanding of many things in the world, as narrative is the foundational structure of how we make sense of the world. Imagine that you are in possession of an object and your friend has no idea what this object is. How do you explain the function of this object? Clearly, it is possible to tell your friend the name of this object. You tell your friend the object is called a "hemasa." However, what explanation does the name really give? The name provides no context for the object's purpose. It is likely that you create a story around the object, explaining its function, why and how it is used, who uses the object, and in what context it is used. Here, you have created a verbal explanation about an unknown object, utilizing narrative to explain what it is. In the narratives we create about ourselves, we are doing the same thing, however with an object that is much more important: ourselves.

When we think about agency, about *doing* things in the world and making specific changes, this doing is intrinsically tied to the two factors that makes us human: the mind and the body. The mind is an agent, in that our ideas will shape and influence those around us (and vice versa) while it is the body that physically enacts those ideas. Western philosophy has been shaped by the distinction between the mind and the body. However, we must consider how these two work together to create and enact agency. Let us consider the position of Letitia Meynell (Campbell and Meynell 2010), who outlines the significant gap in philosophical studies of agency caused by the erasure of the body. For Meynell, "the human body *is* an agent, inevitably transforming through its actions both the world and itself" (1; emphasis in original). We must, therefore, consider the role of the body in our analysis of agency, identity, and narrative. For those subjects marginalized by the course of history and ideology, the body is the lynchpin for said marginalization. We need to conceptualize this marginalized position in order to more fully and richly understand agency as both a theoretical concept and a lived reality. When we talk about the role of bodies in agency, we are more specifically talking about the role of lived experience (versus theoretical supposition) in our daily lives. Following Meynell, "re-envisioning knowledge, morality, and politics as grounded in living, marked, diverse, active bodies and addressing ongoing conversations from this robust physical and political basis" (11) will help us to understand more fully the important connection between embodiment and agency.

When we consider the relationship between identity and agency, it is important to consider the role different identities have in constructing and enacting our agentic possibilities. This is where embodiment ties in to our current discussion. Embodied, lived experience is always relative; it differs greatly depending on a subject's position in the world. And this position is influenced by identities or identity traits that are chosen and those that are not. For example, one cannot choose their native language. This is an identity with us from birth. This is not to say, however, that these identities are immutable or static. Other identities are adopted by subjects and are used (as are those identities that follow us from birth) to express to others our values, positions, and ideals. These identities include political views, ideological stances, even musical tastes. Both categories of identity possess agentic possibilities.

I distinguish between these two types of identity not to establish a hierarchy but rather to emphasize the importance of embodiment in our understanding of agency. Owing to our differing identities and experiences, we will understand and interpret the world in different ways. One's age, gender, socioeconomic standing, race, religion, and the like will shape how one views the world and how the world views them. This does not mean we cannot share experiences, values, and goals, but rather the example illustrates how lived bodies are a locus for our experiences in the world. If agency is what we do and identity is who we are, then we are obligated to consider the body's role in agency and identity.

How Do Narratives Influence Our Concepts of Identity and Agency?

As previously stated, we use narrative to create meaning in our world, while narrative simultaneously shapes our world. If narrative is a way in which we shape our experiences into a meaningful representation of our world, how do narrative constructs of the world impact us as individuals? This is an important question, as dominant narratives shape how we understand the world. In this section, we will explore how narratives shape us as subjects. We will briefly detour into a discussion of ideology in order to explore the impact of Louis Althusser's understanding of the relationship between identity, agency, and ideology. Specifically, we will consider the important effects of Althusser's analysis of the educational apparatus for our dialogue surrounding narrative, agency, and scholarly identity.

One of the key ways we begin to understand our identity or our place in the world is when we enter school. For many young children, the classroom is the first time they make meaningful connections with people outside of their close family. In the classroom, students learn fundamental tools, such as reading and writing, but they also learn important social skills, such as managing conflict and creating friendships. We are shaped, in many ways, by our experience in this institution. However, the ways in which school as an institution shapes subjects are never neutral or objective. If we consider Althusser's argument that school functions as an ideological apparatus, we begin to understand the implications this institution has upon agency and identity. An ideological apparatus is, in essence, any institution that shapes specific values for its citizens. These can take the form of the school, law, religion, or family, to name a few examples. The school, as an ideological apparatus, is united under a particular ideology. Here, we can understand ideology as a set of values that shape our experience of the world.

For Althusser, who follows a Marxist tradition focusing on class struggles, the school is a place in which the ideology of the ruling class is constantly reinforced in subtle ways. From the material that is presented in class to the ways in which we are taught to behave in the classroom, these practices follow in line with the ideology of a ruling class. While the implications of Althusser's understanding of the school as an ideological apparatus may exude an Orwellian air of dystopia, these practices are typically not overt. They are subtly introduced and reiterated throughout our classroom experience, usually without our noticing that it occurs. Let us look at an example to better illustrate the idea of the school as an ideological apparatus. Think about the various history courses you took in high school. It is highly likely that your history classes focused upon the United States and Western Europe. Did you take a class on Latin American history? Were you offered a course on Latin American history? Perhaps you say, well, US history is relevant because we are in the United States, and Western European history has an important impact on US history. However, so too does Latin American history.

The history of the United States is intrinsically tied to Latin America, from Hernando de Soto's explorations of Alabama in 1540 to the Mexican-American War, which shaped geographically a large part of the western United States. Consider the right-wing dictatorships of Central America in the 1980s, which were largely backed and supported by the US government. When we realize that certain areas of history are emphasized in school and others are relatively ignored, we begin to see how certain values are imposed and sustained by the school as an ideological apparatus. Our educational experience has been shaped by a particular ideology. If we understand the school as an ideological apparatus, as something that shapes our values and our identities, this brings up important questions for the concept of agency we have developed throughout this chapter. How can we have agency if the school, as an ideological institution, shapes who we are? What then, is the role of agency?

That our experience in school shapes particular values and ideologies over others does not revoke our agency. When we become aware of the specific ideologies that institutions reinforce, we can begin to question the value of these viewpoints for our own specific worldview. If, following Althusser, "ideology represents the imaginary relationship of individuals to their real conditions of existence" (2006, 109), we need only become aware of the real conditions of our existence. These conditions, in opposition to the concrete ideologies supported by instruction in school, are variant, subjective, and always in flux. They will never be the same for any group of people, as the experiences of people are always varied and different. We enact agency in our acceptance or rejection of the ideologies imposed by the school as an institution. When we become aware of dominant ideologies as constructs, as things that reflect their own ideology and values rather than any inherent truth, only then are we able to challenge these ideas. This leads us to our final question for this chapter: What impact does this have for you as a college student?

The Importance of Developing a Scholarly Voice

You are part of a scholarly community. Each of you possesses unique ideas and perspectives that you will share with your scholarly community and with the world outside of the university. Your ideas are important, as are the ways in which you express these ideas. Here we come to the significance of developing a scholarly voice. A scholarly voice blends your ideas and perspectives with your particular ways of expressing these ideas. One technique for developing a scholarly voice is to read authors you admire. However, I offer a word of caution: do not let the scholarly voices of others overtake your own. Glean from others techniques that you like, but adapt them to your own voice and to your own perspective. Let them provide the brush that you use to paint your own picture. Your scholarly voice is the tool that you will use to communicate your ideas to the world. The formation of a scholarly voice is also an act of identity construction. We utilize our scholarly voices to tell people who we are. We share our values and our opinions through our scholarly voices. Through our scholarly voices we create narratives about who we are as scholars. If narrative is a principal way that we make sense of our world, we communicate that understanding to others and create communities around this understanding.

Your scholarly voice will not echo alone in isolated chambers. Through this voice, you will begin to forge connections with other scholars. As we have seen, narrative is tied to questions of identity and identification. Narrative is a way of communicating who we are as individuals and creating community upon the basis of how we identify ourselves. Returning to the question of agency, never forget that creating narrative is an act of agency. It is creating and claiming space for yourself. Your scholarly voice is a narrative act of identity and agency. It is how you construct yourself as a scholar and how you use that identity to enact change. There is a particular urgency in the creation of a scholarly voice. This is not to say that it must be done quickly or immediately, but rather the urgency lies in the great impact that your scholarly voice has, not only for yourself, but for wider-reaching communities, both within the university and outside of it.

Conclusions

Consider for a moment the narrative we have constructed throughout this chapter. We began with an introduction; developed the central concepts of agency, identity, and narrative; considered the larger implications these concepts have for developing a scholarly voice; and now we reach a conclusion.

However, we spent a great deal of time exploring the idea that our notion of self is always in flux. It changes, adapts, and reshapes itself through the various experiences we have in our lives. Therefore, can this narrative really conclude? Structurally, yes. In a few lines I will stop writing, and you will stop reading. Yet this does not signal the end our narrative journey. It is my hope that the narrative of this chapter—that is, the story of the interplay between agency, identity, and narrative—will help you to shape your scholarly voice. The best conclusion for these concepts is none at all. Rather, it is my aim that this chapter plays into Austin's performative. Beyond saying something, this chapter must *do* something. And what this chapter contributes to your journey as college student is, ultimately, up to you and your ever-evolving narrative.

Works Cited

Althusser, L. (2006). *Lenin and philosophy and other essays.* Delhi, India: Aakar Books.

Anderson, H. (2008). *Conversation, language, and possibilities: A postmodern approach to therapy.* New York, NY: Basic Books.

Austin, J. L. (1975). *How to do things with words.* Cambridge, MA: Harvard University Press.

Bal, M. (2009). *Narratology: Introduction to the theory of narrative.* Canada: University of Toronto Press.

Bamberg, M. (2009). Identity and narration. In P. Hühn, J. Pier, W. Schmid, & J. Schönert (Eds.), *Handbook of narratology* (pp. 132–143). Berlin, Germany: Walter de Gruyter.

Butler, J. (1993). *Bodies that matter: On the discursive limits of "sex."* New York, NY: Routledge.

Campbell, S, & Maynell, L. (Eds.). (2009). *Embodiment and agency.* University Park, PA: Penn State University Press.

Holland, D., Lachicotte, W., Jr., Skinner, D., & Cain, C. (2001). *Identity and agency in cultural worlds.* Cambridge, MA: Harvard University Press.

Korsgaard, C. M. (2009). *Self-constitution: Agency, identity, and integrity.* United Kingdom: Oxford University Press.

Mackenzie, C. (2009). Personal Identity, Narrative Integration, and Embodiment. In S. Campbell & L. Maynell (Eds.), *Embodiment and agency* (pp. 100-125). University Park, PA: Penn State University Press.

Introduction to Chapter 7

ONE OF THE most important things you can involve yourself in is undergraduate research. The opportunities that this will open up for you as a student, graduate student, and professional are boundless. There is no telling what I could be doing with my life right now had I taken advantage of research opportunities as an undergraduate student. Dr. Anneliese Bolland and Dr. Kim Bissell have put together a great introductory chapter about research and its importance to society. They present definitions and case studies that allow the reader to engage in examples that highlight the importance of sound research.

The authors describe the need for research in society, discuss the importance of being a good consumer of research, and, finally, walk us through how to ask a research question. Becoming an engaged scholar will make you a better student, citizen, and professional. It will allow you to work on your critical thinking skills, and test theories and ideas in new and different ways.

I am thankful that Dr. Bolland and Dr. Bissell have joined this project and have asked that you join them on their journey to find answers to the questions of our lives.

CHAPTER 7

Foundations of Social Research

Finding Meaning and Perspective
in the Research Process

Anneliese Bolland and Kim Bissell

Introduction: What Is Research, and How Do I Consume Research?

As WE THINK about understanding and participating in research in society, one thing we might ask ourselves is "how many questions have I asked today?" followed by "what was the process that I used to come to an answer to any particular question?" One question that each of you recently asked was "where should I attend college?" What process did you use to reach that decision? To come to an answer, you had to collect **data** or **information**. Administrative information such as cost of tuition and cost of meal plans are examples of data that you might have used. Scholarship opportunities might have played into your decision-making process. Some of you might have interviewed people, such as family and friends or even strangers, asking for their opinions, attitudes, or experiences. Some of you might have consulted pictures of campus or the city to help you make a decision. What about the availability of a certain major or the notoriety of a specific faculty member who you might want to be mentored by? Ultimately, there might have been one source of information or several sources of information that you used to help you answer the question "where should I attend college?" In any case, you identified a question and then used a process to answer that question.

Research happens around us constantly, and it can take many forms. Many of us were introduced to research in an elementary school science class and were encouraged to (or made to) participate in a science fair, where we learned what a hypothesis is (it actually goes beyond an "educated guess") and learned the "five steps to research" (there are actually more). If you participated in a school science fair, you participated in research. It is likely that you have participated in research more than you are aware of because often research such as making a decision about where to attend college happens informally.

Research is all around us. Be mindful about the next magazine article, news story, or website you read where the words "a study proves that" are present. **Popular press** sources identifying relationships between variables should be approached with caution. You'll often find these somewhat suspect relationships touted in a sexy headline such as, for example, an article in the Huffington Post, updated in January 2017: "A Glass of Red Wine is the Equivalent to an Hour at the Gym, Says New Study." We would encourage you to become critical consumers of research. When you see headlines such as these, investigate the actual research study that has led to such a headline (Dolinsky et al. 2012; Stich 2017).

Before we present the first case study, first we should establish a definition of **research**. While it's a little challenging to come up with a succinct definition, we can establish research as a process. It is a process of asking questions and answering those questions. If there is a question to ask, there is, inherently, a problem to be solved. Now, all problems are not created equally. For example, hunger is a huge problem for some individuals while it is a mere fleeting problem for others. Solving this problem, for both of these sides of the same coin involve research. I might use a research method (or several methods) to try to solve the problem or answer the question of global hunger in children. Alternatively, I might use a research method to figure out where I want to go to dinner tonight. Again, research is a process, and it is a process that can change throughout the process, and in many cases, should change throughout the process. This willingness to adapt the process of research is crucial. As new knowledge is created and more understanding is present, our approaches to solving problems should change. This can occur over years or through a semester.

It is with the simple definition of research (i.e., the process of asking and answering questions) that we will move forward through this chapter. In this chapter, we approach the process of research through four case studies where we will present the issues we feel are most critical to understanding research in society using examples that are relatable. In each of these case studies, we discuss why research is important and how to ask the right questions, how to ensure that ethical principles guide the research process, and how to use theory to frame research. In each of these case studies, we also discuss some of the results of these projects and how these results both acknowledge limitations in research and guide future research.

Works Cited

Dolinsky, V. W., Jones, K. E., Sidhu, R. S., Haykowsky, M., Czubryt, M. P., Gordon, T., & Dyck, J. R. (2012). Improvements in skeletal muscle strength and cardiac function induced by resveratrol during exercise training contribute to enhanced exercise performance in rats. *Journal of Physiology, 590*(11), 2783–2799.

Stich, D.M. (2017). A glass of red wine is equivalent to an hour at the gym, says new study. *Huffington Post*. Retrieved from http://www.huffingtonpost. co.uk/2016/01/08/a-glass-of-red-wine-is-the-equivalent-to-an-hour-at-the-gym- says-new-study_n_7317240.html

Mobile Youth and Poverty Study

Why is Research Important?

Evidence has been already found that growing up poor can have long-lasting effects. Many researchers have studied poverty from different perspectives, including health, education, criminal justice, sociology, and more.

Disparities between the poor and non-poor have been found in many areas, including health, education, criminal justice, and others. Health disparities have been defined as differences that are potentially avoidable and unjust, placing socio-economically disadvantaged groups at risk for poor health (Whitehead 1991, 219; Braveman 2006, 180). Moreover, examining health disparities using a life-course perspective (Braveman 2014) suggests that unjust earlier events or conditions (e.g., during childhood) can create later health disparities (e.g., during adulthood); changing these earlier events or conditions (e.g., through better education) can prevent poor health later in life by removing a person from a socially disadvantaged class.

Asking the Right Research Questions
Significance

In the case of poverty, the sky is the limit in terms of research questions. Often guiding the research questions when there is such a broad area of study are three things: (a) interests of the researcher(s), (b) a call for proposals to fund a specific area of research, and/or (c) the availability of existing data.

Let's first take the interests of the researcher(s). I tell my students this and remind myself of this all the time: If a topic is not **personally significant**, I will not have too much luck with the research process itself; I certainly might get bored with it quickly, and my work won't be its best. Personal significance can mean just an interest, although it can also go deeper than that as well. I could have been personally affected by an experience that has now influenced my desire and ability to conduct research in that area. Any research study that is undertaken should also have **theoretical significance** and **social significance**. What do I mean by these two things? First, a research study should generate knowledge. This may happen in its contribution to theory. This suggests that I need to approach my research with a **theoretical framework** in mind. There are a lot of established theories already in existence. I might want to take a theory and see if it applies to my specific research circumstances or population of interest. I should have some logic or reason to believe that two constructs (or more) are related or that one variable might predict another. There should be, for example, some rationale for that relationship or prediction. Finally, any research that you undertake should have **social significance**. All research should benefit society in some way. This benefit does not have to be direct (although it may be), but could be in the knowledge that is generated.

Decisions, Decisions, Decisions: Study Design

Many decisions go into a research study before any data are actually collected. In 1998, one year of funding was granted to John Bolland, of the University of Alabama, to conduct a survey in Mobile, Alabama, with adolescents who lived in underclass neighborhoods. For a discussion of the term *underclass*, see Wilson, Myrdal, and Massey and Denton (Wilson 1987; Myrdal 1962; Massey and Denton 1993). In order to conduct the survey, students were recruited to participate in an internship where they would learn about research and collect data in Mobile over the summer. Participants were to be paid ten dollars for their time to complete the survey. Decisions had to be made about (a) what items to include on the **survey**, (b) what neighborhoods would be targeted for **participant recruitment**, (c) how to **recruit** participants, and (d) how to **administer the survey**. Each of these areas are quite important to think through, weighing pros and cons before beginning data collection.

Ethics

There were considerable ethical principles to consider in the Mobile Youth and Poverty Study. One of the primary ethical areas of concern was that the population—adolescents—is considered a **special population**. Not only were the researchers proposing to study humans, but they were also proposing to study minors, or those under the age of eighteen in the state of Alabama (in 1998, those under nineteen were considered minors, needing parental consent to participate in research). Therefore, parental or caregiver consent had to be obtained for each participant in the study. Next, some of the questions on the Mobile Youth Survey asked participants to reveal whether they had engaged in risky behaviors such as alcohol or drug use. Because of the nature of these questions, it was very important that the participants' privacy was considered. Because there were hopes that this survey would continue beyond just one year (making it **longitudinal**), the researchers wanted to collect identifying information from the participants. Thus, **anonymity** was not promised to the participants, but **confidentiality** was promised. All identifying information is kept in a data file separate from the participants' survey responses. Thus, no attempts are made by anyone analyzing the survey data to identify any one, single individual. Also, participants were told that they could skip any question that made them feel uncomfortable. Finally, before any parents were contacted about their children participating in this study, approval from the institution's **Institutional Review Board (IRB)** was sought and granted.

What Comes Next?

As I mentioned, the Mobile Youth Survey was initially funded for just one year, but after the one year of data collection, Dr. Bolland wrote additional grant proposals to continue data collection. Many of these proposals were funded, resulting in fourteen years of data collection over the summers. That is, for fourteen years, college student interns, both undergraduate and graduate, traveled to Mobile, Alabama, to help conduct the Mobile Youth Survey.

These data have also been used to write academic journal articles (over sixty!), often with researchers from different disciplines collaborating on one paper. I've come back to that idea of a theoretical framework here briefly to provide an example of one study that was done, analyzing the Mobile Youth Survey data, involving collaborators from different disciplines. One theory that is often applicable to the research questions that we want to ask and answer with Mobile Youth and Poverty Study data is Bronfenbrenner's (1986) ecological systems theory. This theory suggests that there are synergistic relationships in a child's environment, where a child exists in a family or home environment but also in a school environment, a neighborhood environment, and even in a larger social or cultural environment. These environments interact to ultimately influence the child's life, including behavior and psychological well-being. This was the framework that we used to investigate both school and community connectedness and how delinquency might play a part in those feelings of belonging (Bolland et al. 2016).

Mobile Youth and Poverty Study data continue to be analyzed with respect to health (Byck et al. 2015), education (Bolland et al. 2017), and criminal justice (Spano and Bolland 2013) disparities. Further, proposals requesting funding to analyze these data and for new data collection continue to be written. This is one example of a study where researchers from almost any discipline can work together to address disparities among one of America's most vulnerable populations.

Works Cited

Bolland, A. C., Tomek, S. E., Besnoy, K. D., & Bolland, J. M. (2017). Gifted 'n the 'hood: Gender and giftedness as predictors of social risk among low-income students. *Exceptionality*, 1–19.

Bolland, K. A., Bolland, J. M., Tomek, S., Devereaux, R. S., Mrug, S., & Wimberly, J. C. (2016). Trajectories of adolescent alcohol use by gender and early initiation status. *Youth & Society, 48*(1), 3–32.

Braveman, P. (2006). Health disparities and health equity: Concepts and measurement. *Annual Review of Public Health, 27*, 167–194.

Braveman, P. (2014). What is health equity: And how does a life-course approach take us further toward it? *Maternal and Child Health Journal, 18*(2), 366–372.

Bronfenbrenner, U. (1986). Ecology of the family as a context for human development: Research perspectives. *Developmental Psychology, 22*(6), 723–742.

Byck, G. R., Bolland, J. M., Dick, D., Swann, G., Henry, D., & Mustanski, B. (2015). Effect of housing relocation and neighborhood environment on adolescent mental and behavioral health. *Journal of Child Psychology and Psychiatry, 56*(11), 1185–1193.

Massey, E. K., Gebhardt, W. A., & Garnefski, N. (2008). Adolescent goal content and pursuit: A review of the literature from the past 16 years. *Developmental Review, 28*(4), 421–460. doi: https://doi.org/10.1016/j.dr.2008.03.002

Myrdal, G. (1962). *Challenge to affluence: The emergence of an under-class.* New York, NY: Pantheon Books.

Spano, R., & Bolland, J. M. (2013). Disentangling the effects of violent victimization, violent behavior, and gun carrying for minority innercity youth living in extreme poverty. *Crime and Delinquency, 59*(2), 191–213.

Whitehead, M. (1991). The concepts and principles of equity and health. *Health Promotion International, 6*(3), 217–228.

Wilson, W. J. (1987). *The truly disadvantaged: The inner city, the underclass, and public policy.* Illinois: University of Chicago Press.

Children, Media Use, and Health

Asking the Right Research Questions

Childhood obesity has been a topic of conversation among health educators, public health officials, teachers, and parents for several decades, and now, children themselves. Childhood obesity is a complex health issue because the causes of weight gain in younger children can be attributed to many factors, such as the child's health behaviors, the home environment, genetics, and, increasingly, a child's social environment (CDC 2016). For mass communication and health communication researchers, this can be the **study topic**. But, if we say we are going to do a research study looking at the influence of the media on childhood obesity, we may be setting ourselves up for a research project that could take a lifetime to complete.

How do we work through the process of narrowing down the topic into something more manageable? The first step is always to look at the previous research from studies that are similar. Use those previous findings as a way of eliminating questions or topics that have been studied extensively and as a way of gauging what questions have yet to be asked. In our study of health and children, the previous research and existing literature is vast and spans decades, so the key becomes identifying what is most relevant and/or pertinent to the study at hand. By starting with a summary of **previous research**, it becomes easier to narrow my interests to a specific research topic. More importantly, am I interested in understanding the causes of obesity or overweight in children, meaning do I want to identify how the X predicts the Y? Or, am I more interested in understanding how several factors, like time spent with the media, the content of that media, and may be BMI, are related? What I want to learn from the study will dictate the **study design**. If I am interested in understanding the causal relationship among variables, I will need to conduct an **experiment**. If I am more interested in understanding how variables are related or correlated, I may conduct a **survey** or an **observational study**.

Arriving to this point of the process means I can start to **develop research questions and hypotheses**. What's the difference and why would I choose one over the other? The general rule of thumb is that if a good bit of research has already been done on the topic and there is a general understanding of how variables might be related to one another, I can move forward with **developing a hypothesis**. What should I be considering as I write a hypothesis?

1. The hypothesis should be a statement rather than a question.
2. The statement should be clear, and it should be obvious what your **independent** and **dependent variables** are.

A **research question (RQ)** is often used when there is less existing literature to guide our predictions. In fact, RQs are more common when we are still trying to figure out if X and Y are even related. Your research question should still guide the research project and assist in the construction of a logical argument, but rather than saying X *will* be related to Y in this way, you are asking *how* X related to Y.

If we return to the example of doing a research project investigating the role of media in childhood obesity, we do have to acknowledge that care should be taken to ensure we, as researchers, are being **ethical**. Whenever you are conducting a study with people, you have to take extra steps to ensure each person is kept safe and that the information they provide to you is kept confidential (if that is how your study is designed). Researchers who are conducting studies with people as their subjects have to submit their projects for review to the IRB. Any student or faculty member at a university or college will have an IRB office to review their study procedures and protocol.

After working through the narrowing down of a topic for research and determining the type of study I want to conduct, I also have to consider the **role of theory** in the research that I am doing. It is important to note that in some fields, often the natural sciences, theory is not used. Theory and theoretical frameworks are more common in the social sciences. Returning to the study of children, media, and health, it could be argued, using the premise of social learning theory (which has evolved into social cognitive theory) that if children observe role models, like parents, eating healthy foods, they are more likely to imitate or model that behavior. Or if applied to the media, if children observe, in a mediated context, healthy behaviors, they are more likely to model those healthy behaviors. In social science studies, the theory may start us at a bigger picture, 30,000 feet in the sky place, and then we use that theory along with our idea to bring our study to something more manageable.

In the social sciences, we often use a **deductive approach**—working from the more general to the specific. We start with a theory, we use that theory to help us develop hypotheses, we observe (collect data), and then we confirm that theory. In other disciplines, an **inductive approach** is used. In this case, we start with the observation, move to the identification of patterns, develop tentative hypotheses, and then develop a theory from that. There is no right or wrong way to use theory; however, it is important to understand if theory is relevant in the field in which you are doing research so it can be woven into your study in an appropriate way.

Another consideration with our **sample** of children or **special populations** is to determine if individuals who have low cognitive skills and/or are lower in literacy can understand any of the questions you have asked. Returning to our question about milk consumption in a day, we could show participants a picture of a glass of milk rather than using words and ask them (rather than asking them to read a question) how much they had that day. While there is never a perfect solution to all of these issues, it is important and even our obligation to not only design a study well but ensure that the data we are getting is valid.

As we think about the design of our study, one of the questions we need to ask ourselves is, "what kind of data do we want?" Do we want numbers that can be run through statistical software? Do we want data that has come from interviews or focus groups? Again, part of the answer to this question will come from considering what it is we want to know. As a part of a study I was doing looking at children's food preferences following exposure to food advertisements, children participating in a child nutrition camp were **randomly sampled** into one of three groups—healthy food ads, unhealthy food ads, and no ads. They were then, one by one, led into a room where the foods being advertised were on a table. Each child was told he/she could pick whatever foods they wanted, and researchers, who were behind a one-way window, recorded the foods they picked. The goal of this was to see how or if the food advertisements prompted the kids to select the foods they had just seen advertised. In this **experiment,** the food advertisement was manipulated (**independent variable),** and the number of food items and the type of food items (healthy or unhealthy) served as the **dependent variable**. It is important to note that prior to exposing children to any food advertisements, we collected data on their food preferences and even asked them how much they liked the exact foods they were going to be shown later.

Survey research is very common for bigger-picture questions when we want to understand how people respond to the same questions (what types of foods do children prefer for snacks—healthy or unhealthy?). Whereas a **survey** allows us to ask questions about media use, food preferences, eating attitudes, or nutritional knowledge, an **experiment** is going to use the same idea and **manipulate** some component of the study to identify if an effect is present (e.g., does exposure to unhealthy food advertisements predict a greater preference for unhealthy foods?).

In order to make a solid case for an **observable effect**, we needed to understand the messages that were being communicated to kids about food. Subsequently, we had to conduct a **content analysis** of food advertisements to know with any assurance what they were actually being exposed to. In another component of this study, we asked children in our child nutrition camp to tell us the television programs they watched the most, and using that information, we recorded all of the programs from a variety of networks throughout the day for a week to then analyze all of the ads that were shown during each program. Findings from this **content analysis** allowed us to say with greater confidence that children who spent more time watching television each day were also more likely to be exposed to ads for unhealthy foods. In this case, the **content analysis** helped us set up the second study, the **experiment** of food advertisements and children's food preferences.

After conducting our research, the next important step is figuring out what to do with all of the data collected, or **making sense of the numbers**. If you have conducted **quantitative research**, you will be dealing with numbers that will be run through any number of statistical software packages like R, SPSS, or SAS. In a recent study examining whether general media was use while eating—and if so, how much—and if familial media use during mealtimes related to a child's general understanding of health, descriptive statistics were first run to tell us basic information such as how many boys and girls we had in the study, what the ethnic background was for all participants, how much time in general they spent using media during the day, and what their general level of nutritional knowledge was via a single score.

This type of data or these types of statistics are called **univariate statistics** when you are only looking at a single number, such as the percentage of girls in the sample or the nutritional knowledge score. When you want to take your findings to the next level, you start looking at **multivariate statistics**, which means you are looking at a relationship between multiple variables. In the Bissell, Baker, et al (2017), the researchers used regression analysis (a statistical process for estimating the relationship among variables) which indicated a significant, inverse relationship between time spent watching media (television, internet, and video games) and nutritional knowledge, meaning the more time a child spent using media during the day, the lower the child's nutritional knowledge score was. In this particular study, very few **statistically significant** findings were identified when examining each child's use of social media and the various **dependent variables**. While we could chalk this up to not supporting a hypothesis, the lack of statistical support should also push us to question why the findings were not significant. In some cases, the **sample size** is too small for a statistically significant finding to emerge; in other cases, it is possible the relationship just doesn't exist, or, more to the point, in the case of second- and third-grade children, maybe not enough of them used social media to be a blip on the statistical radar. This does not mean we ignore the findings but rather we consider what we could do differently if we were to replicate the study. Of great importance is thinking through rationale explanations for all of the findings—statistically significant or not. As stated earlier, nonsignificant findings can be as important as statistically significant ones.

It is the hope of your professors that as you start to pursue a path in research you'll find a topic that is interesting to you, engaging, and most importantly, one you will be passionate about. Sometimes the research requirements for a class do not always align with this line of thinking, but if you are doing research as part of your career or job, it is hoped that you'll land on a topic that challenges you to keep asking questions. It is important to know that research can come in a variety of forms and be used in a variety of ways. Regardless of the type of research you do and regardless of the home you find for your research, it is important to know that you are creating knowledge with what you are doing. Each study and each set of findings helps grow our understanding of your topic.

Works Cited

Bandura, A. (1977). *Social Learning Theory.* Englewood Cliffs, NJ: Prentice Hall.

Bandura, A., Ross, D., & Ross, S. A., (1961). Transmission of aggression through imitation of aggressive models. *Journal of Abnormal and Social Psychology, 63*(3), 575–582.

Bissell, K., Baker, K., Pember, S., Bissell, K., Zhang, X., & Yang, Y. (2017). The role of media use and family media use in children's eating behaviors, food preferences, and health literacy. Paper presented to the *Mass Communication & Society Division* at the annual meeting of the Association for Education in Journalism and Mass Communication. Chicago, IL.

Bissell, K., Conlin, M. L., Zhang, X., Bie, B., & McLemore, D. (2017). Let go of my iPad: Testing the effectiveness of new media technologies to measure children's food intake and eating behavior. *Mass Communication and Society,* 1–25.

CDC (Centers for Disease Control and Prevention). (2011). *School health guidelines to promote healthy eating and physical activity* (Morbidity and Mortality Weekly Report, Recommendations and Reports, 60(5). Retrieved from https://www.cdc.gov/healthyschools/npao/pdf/MMWR-School-Health-Guidelines.pdf

CDC (Centers for Disease Control and Prevention). (2016). *The social-ecological model: A framework for prevention.* Retrieved from http://www.cdc.gov/ViolencePrevention/overview/social-ecologicalmodel.html

Fanelli, D. (2009). How many scientists fabricate and falsify research? A systematic review and meta-analysis of survey data. *PLOS.* DOI: https://doi.org/10.1371/journal.pone.0005738

McLeroy, K. R., Bibeau, D., Steckler, A., & Glanz, K. (1988). An ecological perspective on health promotion programs. *Health Education & Behavior, 15*(4), 351–377.

Stokols, D. (1996). Translating social ecological theory into guidelines for community health promotion. *American Journal of Health Promotion, 10*(4), 282–298.

Research in the Natural Sciences

We've had the opportunity to discuss research in a few different areas and discuss the way we move from a general interest or idea to a solid research project. We've discussed ways we can examine poverty from a variety of perspectives, ways to study children and health, and a variety of ways research projects can evolve organically from those topics. With that being said, we recognize that not all of you will be interested in the social sciences and may drift more to the **natural sciences**. This next case study will give you a chance to see how a natural science research project comes together while also looking at the ways components of the research will be different.

Again, we begin with a study topic, . Researchers in biology, marine biology, marine conservation, and ecology are all struggling with the issue of coral reef bleaching or the degradation of coral reefs, especially in areas like off the coast of Australia where more than 2,900 individual reefs and more than 900 islands stretch over 1,400 miles to make up the Great Barrier Reef. From afar, we hear of the Great Barrier Reef located in the Coral Sea and envision turquoise waters and beautiful reefs with unusual plant and animal species. However, the Great Barrier Reef lost half of its coral in approximately thirty years (De'ath et al. 2012). To put this into context, think about half of the Grand Canyon crumbing to ruins in less than three decades, or think about Yellowstone's geysers shriveling up and going away in just a few short years. Reefs around the world are experiencing a rapid decline because of increased threats from pollution and climate change. Now that we have established a problem, let's try to understand how questions lead to study design. As we have done with the previous case studies, it is important to refer to the **previous research** and **background literature** for context to see what **appropriate questions** might be relevant. In our natural sciences case study—coral reef degradation—let's review some of the background information:

Lizard Island is a continental island located in the northern section of the Great Barrier Reef. However, recent environmental disturbances are having detrimental effects on coral reef ecosystems around the world, and specifically on Lizard Island. Coral reefs are extremely sensitive to threats of climate change, natural disturbances (e.g., cyclones, hurricanes) and crown-of-thorns starfish (*Acanthaster planci*) outbreaks. Climate change poses several threats that have already severely influenced coral communities. Events such as sea level rise, ocean acidification, and temperature-induced coral bleaching are all associated effects of the current state of global warming. Further, declines in coral cover also can impact fish biodiversity (Jones et al. 2004) as declines in fish biodiversity are related to water quality and the ocean's ability to provide food (Worm et al. 2006).

This summary of previous research tells us that specific marine communities may be declining or at least are affected because of a variety of natural and man-made factors. So, let's dive deeper into the research to see what's already been studied.

The chaetodontid fish community is strongly tied to coral reefs as a source of nutrition and as habitat for juvenile recruits (Pratchett, Hoey, and Wilson 2014). Scleractinian coral make up the primary food source for most butterflyfish species, so there is a close association between butterflyfish and coral reefs (Pratchett 1995). They are, therefore, a model group of organisms for studying the relationships between coral and reef fishes. A study in 2001 (Grossman 2001) compared the niche separation of two species of butterflyfish found on Lizard Island: *Chaetodon auriga* and *Chaetodon vagabundus* (Lizard Island Research Station, n.d.). This study compared recruitment levels, competition, and resource partitioning between the two species across three habitat zones of fringing reefs. The study's results show a relationship between habitat, zoning, and subsequent abundance of both species of butterflyfish. The larger class size of both species preferred coral habitat zones compared to coral rubble and rubble zones whereas smaller-sized fish of both species preferred the coral rubble zones. This implies meaningful interactions between pre- and postrecruitment settlement and habitat, linking fish populations to habitat availability. *Chaetodontidae* often exhibit different spatial patterns throughout a reef, and patterns may be structured by competition for limiting resources, such as the preferred food of coral polyps. Fish with similar diets tend to occupy the same feeding niche and could be in competition with one another, exhibiting interspecific competition, and the coexistence amongst several species is maintained by resource partitioning.

Abundance and distribution are closely tied to the optimal niche of a species. Generalist species can survive over a wide range of resources, habitats and conditions, whereas specialists require specific conditions, and specific prey species and habitats, and they have very narrow distributions (Bean, Jones, and Caley 2002). Specialists are much more constrained by the availability of resources and are less able to cope with changes in resource availability compared to generalists (Pratchett 2014). Specialization does not necessarily refer to one species or one genera of coral in this study. Specialization refers to the general prey type and source of nutrition: hard coral, soft coral, invertebrates, and turf algae. In a severely coral-degraded reef where a key structural component and ideal food resource for many coral-feeding fish is lacking, interspecific interactions are likely to be challenged and this stressful condition can generate the switch from specialists to generalists in coral dependent fish.

Now that we know what some of the previous research has examined and what the results from this previous research are, it is easier to formulate relevant questions. The easy question from the above information is, how exactly is this happening and can anything be done to stop it? We can take this a step further and ask an even more specific, **testable research question** as it pertains to the effects of this decline in coral reefs by asking the following question: What are the effects of recent coral degradation on the population and feeding behavior of certain species of butterflyfish common to a mid-shelf patch reef off of Lizard Island? In this case, the researcher is taking a specific species common to coral reefs—the butterflyfish—and looking for trends on coral cover, fish population density, and foraging and grouping behaviors—on a specific island within the Great Barrier Reef (Bissell 2017).

Our more specific research questions ask about trends in coral cover, fish population density, and fish behavior following two category IV cyclones that hit Lizard Island within eleven months of each other. The researcher in this case is wanting to better understand the effects of these two environmental disturbances, but the researcher does not have "pre-data"—or data collected on the coral cover, population density, and fish behavior prior to the cyclones—so the researcher has to rely on data collected by other scientists to fill in those gaps. This is one of the many ways research in the natural sciences is very different from social sciences because in the social sciences, each researcher has to collect his/her own pre- and post-data.

In the natural sciences, we are concerned with the description, prediction, and understanding of natural phenomena based on observation and empirical evidence, and in the **social sciences,** we are more concerned with society and the relationships among individuals within a society. In short, we are dealing with tremendously more variability when dealing with humans than when we are dealing with, say, fish or coral.

Back to our study of coral reef degradation: we know that we want to look at three specific things related to butterflyfish following two massive cyclones that swept through the area. How would we go about answering these questions we have about population density, feeding patterns, and grouping behavior? Using the guidance of the Pratchett (1995) research and similar other research, our natural science researcher proposed the following: The study organisms that were observed were of the family *Chaetodontidae*. Butterflyfish were selected for observation because they are diurnally active and observer tolerant, and were found to be relatively abundant and species rich during preliminary observations. Substrate data was collected using a 30 m tape along the reef out front of the research station. Thirty transects were established perpendicular to the shore going across the reef with at least 10m of buffer between each transect. Substrate data of coral cover was collected using a point intercept transect, and data was recorded every 50 cm totaling 60 points per transect. The 30 transects covered 900 square meters of Casuarina Reef, a reef that was once largely dominated by even more massive corals as well as staghorn *Acroporas* and *Pocillopora* hard coral. Abundance data was collected for ten species of butterflyfish using timed swims across the reef, perpendicular to the shore and similar to the collection of substrate data. A visual belt census was conducted during the timed swim of three minutes, with a 2-meter width of the belt for fish counts. Thirty replicates were performed, covering 900 square meters of the reef without doubling back, and the census was conducted in the same territories as the substrate surveys. Eight of the ten observed species of butterflyfish were chosen for continued observation of their feeding patterns and grouping habits.

Confused? No worries. Most of us would be. One of the goals for any researcher in the natural sciences is to ensure that all material is written in a way that can be understood by the average person. If what you just read was not understandable, that is because that information came from the study's **methods** section, which is about the only place you can really write above most people's heads. In the methods section, you have to provide **precision** so that if other researchers wanted to **replicate** your study, they would be able to do so by following the **procedures** in the methods section. The study described above is considered **field research**. One of the exciting propositions of research in the natural sciences is that depending on what you study, you can go out into the field to collect your data rather than sitting in a lab—although some scientists love sitting in labs! In the case of our natural science researcher, the "field" just happened to be the Coral Ocean around the Great Barrier Reef.

After spending several weeks collecting data for the above study, our natural science researcher **analyzed the data** in a fashion very similar to what we discussed with our social science research—SPSS. After making comparisons across the transects and analyzing the grouping behaviors of the butterflyfish, the researcher concluded that a relationship existed between habitat, zoning, and subsequent abundance of both species of butterflyfish included in the study. Results from the study further indicated higher densities in population for three of the four observed generalists species, and when compared to data collected ten years previously, a significant decline in the species was identified. The researcher noted that if the coral degradation continued through a combination of natural disasters and pollution, the abundance of specialists of the butterflyfish would decrease significantly, possibly resulting in a loss of the species.

As a researcher in the natural sciences, it is now your job to make this information meaningful and relevant. In this case, the researcher needs to **describe the quantitative results** and **make inferences from the available statistics**.

In the study of the butterflyfish, the natural science researcher was able to draw comparisons from results from previous studies to note if any increase or decrease in population density and grouping behavior was observed or see if feeding patterns were different. In this case, **insignificant findings** would actually be a good finding because it would suggest that maybe the degradation of the coral reefs off Lizard Island was not affecting marine species in a negative way. After writing up the study and presenting findings in a meaningful way, our researcher needs to take it one step further by talking about the practical application of the research. Researchers outside of the natural sciences may look at natural science research and become confused because it seems like what the researchers are dealing with is little more than minutiae. As a researcher, it is your job to help all readers understand the practical application of the findings and help all readers understand the relevance of what is being done. The last step of the research process is **disseminating the findings**. In the case of all research studies, findings can be presented at academic conferences, submitted to academic journals, or even broken down into a press release for an broader reach to the public.

Whatever your outlet for dissemination, make sure your research has been presented in a way that is appropriate and understandable for the target audience.

Works Cited

Bean, K., Jones, G. P., & Caley, M. J. (2002). Relationships among distribution, abundance and microhabitat specialisation in a guild of coral reef triggerfish (family Balistidae). *Marine Ecology Progress Series, 233*, 263–272.

Bissell, K. E. (2017). The effects of coral reef degradation on the butterflyfish (family *Chaetdontidae*) community on a Lizard Island reef: Population density, foraging patterns, and grouping behavior. Paper presented to the SIT Study Abroad Program in Rainforest, Reef, and Cultural Ecology meeting in Cairnes, Australia.

De'ath, G., Fabricius, K. E., Sweatman, H., & Puotinen, M. (2012). The 27–year decline of coral cover on the Great Barrier Reef and its causes. *Proceedings of the National Academy of Sciences, 109*(44), 17995–17999.

Grossman, L. (2001). Niche separation of *Chaetodontid auriga* and *Chaetodontid vagabundus* on a fringing reef at Lizard Island, GBR: Recruitment, competition, and resource partitioning. Unpublished student report. World Learning, Cairns, QLD 4870. Australia.

Jones, G. P., & McCormick, M. I. (2002). Numerical and energetic processes in the ecology of coral reef fishes. In P. F. Sale (Ed.), *Coral reef fishes: Dynamics and diversity in a complex ecosystem* (pp. 221–238). San Diego, CA: Academic Press.

Jones, G. P., McCormick, M. I., Srinivasan, M., & Eagle, J. V. (2004). Coral decline threatens fish biodiversity in marine reserves. *Proceedings of the National Academy of Sciences of the United States of America, 101*(21), 8251–8253.

Lizard Island Research Station (n.d.). Lizard Island Area species list. Unpublished species list.

Pratchett, M. S. (1995). *Spatial distribution, abundance, and diet of butterflyfish (PISCES: Chaetodontidae)* (Doctoral dissertation, Honors Thesis, James Cook University, Townsville, Australia).

Pratchett, M. S. (2014). Feeding preferences and dietary specialization among obligate coral-feeding butterflyfishes. In S. Yabuta & M. L. Berumen (Eds.), *Biology of Butterflyfishes* (pp. 200–225). Boca Raton, FL: CRC Press.

Pratchett, M. S., Hoey, A. S., & Wilson, S. K. (2014). Reef degradation and the loss of critical ecosystem goods and services provided by coral reef fishes. *Current Opinion in Environmental Sustainability, 7*, 37–43.

Worm, B., Barbier, E. B., Beaumont, N., Duffy, J. E., Folke, C., Halpern, B. S., ... & Sala, E. (2006). Impacts of biodiversity loss on ocean ecosystem services. *Science, 314*(5800), 787–790.

Concluding Remarks

We hope that these case studies have illustrated the variety of ways research can be conducted in a variety of disciplines and areas of interest. Hopefully, you've also seen how one area of interest can literally lead to an entire career's worth of research. For us, each time data is collected, new questions arise or new ways of looking at the problem emerge. It is our quest for answers—theoretical and applied—that keep pushing us forward. Even if you don't envision yourself as a career-long researcher, understanding of the role of research in society is crucial because we are surrounded by research in a variety of ways. It is important to be a critical consumer of that information because as you've read, information can sometimes be "spun" in a way that doesn't always reveal all of the facts of findings. Find what interests you; find what you are passionate about and move forward with that as it will help push you through any twenty-page research paper or research project.

Introduction to Chapter 8

I ASKED JESSICA Stershic to write this conclusion from a students' perspective. She has worked tirelessly on reviewing, editing, and tracking down research for this project. She is as familiar with the text as anyone else and seemed like the perfect author to offer final thoughts and conclusions to the project. In true fashion, she jumped at the chance to write this chapter.

Jessica used a critical lens to recap each chapter of the book and added her perspective, or, as she names it, her own "postmodern critique." She encourages readers to develop their own critique of the subjects in the book as well as to develop their own sense of what they think needs a more critical lens. She encourages students to take full advantage of their opportunities both in and out of the classroom. She ends with the idea that we should continue to ask questions of ourselves and issues that we are presented.

I have always felt that a good class, discourse, or reading should ask more questions than it answers. It should be the fuel we need to help us continue to question and progress in life. In that way, Jessica has succeeded!

CHAPTER 8

A Student's Conclusion

Jessica Stershic

YOU HAVE REACHED the end of the book and you think, "great, a conclusion to summarize this project." Typically, I would feel that a conclusion could be skipped because if I actively read the whole book, why do I need a read summary? I will tell you why you need this conclusion.

My name is Jes and I have helped construct, review, and edit this book. Two years ago, I was a freshman and had very little clue about what college had in store for me. Now, I am a junior and, frankly, I do not know what next semester or even next week will be like. I came into college believing that I could think for myself because I could summarize the opinions of others and consume scholarly articles. Let me tell you that I could not think for myself then and I am only recently becoming comfortable with forming my own opinions.

You have heard from many authors in this book and they would all like to help you learn to think. If you are anything like me though, it is hard to imagine yourself as an adult with things to do that aren't homework or hanging out with your friends on Friday nights.

With this conclusion, I will show how I interpreted the chapters and how they intertwine with philosophical concepts.

You probably noticed that the authors put a lot of time into two things: the exercise of thinking and how you can grow as a student by actively questioning the things around you. Instead of accepting the things in front of you, now you should be able to offer an informed critique. This may or may not be a new thought process for you; however, the formal word for our purposes is *postmodernism.*

To understand postmodernism, you need to have a general grip on modernism. Modernism has a long and extensive history; you can read books on that another time. From my extensive (... not) readings on modernism, this is what I came up with: modernism is the current way of thinking that involves popular, accepted, and shared ideas. In addition to ideas, it can also cover philosophy, art, and most activities that involve an opinion. Some characteristics include moving on from past ideas or supportive movements that promote change. Tomes have been written about modernism and postmodernism, so check them out if you are intrigued.

Now think back to high school for a moment. At some point you definitely had a history class with a textbook that seemed impossibly long. You learned what was taught. However, did you ever think about what you were not being taught? Maybe you did but pushed it off because you saw there were only ten minutes until lunch. In this conclusion, though, lunch is much later and we are learning about postmodernism.

What you actually did in that instance was the beginning of a postmodern critique. Other questions you may have also asked were: why wouldn't that topic be taught, does it pose an uncomfortable thought process, will it point out an ugly side of history? You only knew what you were being taught, but we all know there is more to history, or any other topic, than what is typically presented. The things that are just out of sight, those are the beginnings of your postmodern critique.

Now I will take the time to go through each chapter to show you how I dived deeper into what the authors were saying. Along the way, I will pose questions for you to ponder and even explain my opinion. However, the most important pieces of this conclusion are the thoughts you will have while reading.

Engaged Scholarship: In this chapter, the focus is not only on volunteering but thinking about why and for what kind of organization you need to volunteer. The authors talk about college students volunteering to help below-average students in school. Yes, this seems like, and is, a great suggestion for becoming engaged in your community. This would be a modern thought, as volunteering in schools with underperforming children is good. Children are the future of our society so the more support the better. Why wouldn't we all strive to volunteer in a school?

However, the authors then ask "what about our educational systems produces inequalities consistently across students or color and students who are poor"? This is a great question and also a postmodern critique that we are going to explore. Take a moment to ask yourself why our education system does this. We could discuss if it was the school's fault, home life, or other factors.

Then, we can analyze the relationship between the tutor and the child. Your intention is to help the child progress in their studies. By tutoring them, are you enabling them to do better in school or are you creating a dependent child who cannot work without guidance? Even if you are creating a dependent child, are they better off now that they understand more or are they worse off because they are dependent? There isn't an answer that would be the same across all situations, but it does pose some questions that analyze a common situation. Postmodernism would be thinking about these questions and then forming your own opinion.

Critical Thinking Skills: Tindol focuses on how critical thinking can open your world to new views. His emphasis on reading and writing as processes to help put those critical thoughts into action mirror those of many of our authors. College will help you put those ideas into action as well. However, we didn't see him mention those two thoughts together except when he mentioned that if we learn nothing else while in university, we should learn how to read and write. Why? Those two things will help you communicate not only with those in your field but with those who are not.

A modern idea would be that your major helps prepare you for the "real world." If your major and minor were the only ingredients to success, they would teach you how to read and write. Hypothetically, as an engineering student I would then graduate knowing how to read question statements and how to put their answers into a lab report. The problem here is that the emails I send or the presentations I write or the reports I read will not be the same as the lab reports or the problems I have worked with. A postmodern critique of higher education is that you may be prepared to work in your field but you are not ready to communicate with those outside of your field. You will have to take it upon yourself to practice your reading and writing skills. A good way to do this is to read sources that are slightly above your current ability. While you are reading, you will notice how they make you feel a connection between their writing, even if the topic is new to you. Effective writing, and therefore reading, will allow others to feel as passionate about the subject as you are.

Belongingness in Education: Alverson writes that feeling included in a group often has positive effects, not only in the moment but also in other endeavors. With this mindset, schools should encourage students to join groups they most identify with, right? On the surface this seems like a safe and clear notion. Now, let us look at this setting from a racial standpoint. If students feel more included with people who are of the same race, then would encouraging students to attend schools in which their race is dominant be beneficial?

You could say yes or no. From a yes perspective, if people thrive in their best setting, why would you make their setting anything different from the "best it can be"? In this case, it would be a school where the student body is predominantly the same race. Now we have students who are thriving. However, will they feel comfortable working with people of other races in the future? Could you go as far to say that the feelings of inclusion in a racially divided school propagates modern segregation? If the student who is Black has the option of attending the mostly Black school or the mostly White school, could you say there is a wrong and a right answer? (Think for yourself!)

At this point, you should be noticing that modern thoughts have their place in society for a reason, but they may not be the best thoughts for wide practice. Modern thoughts have gained popularity for a variety of reasons, one of them being that they are so ingrained that the initial effort needed to change ways seems too much for people. It is much easier to continue about their day than to try and make a change. Another is that these "rules" benefit most of the population and have for a long time. If most of us walk around concerned only with what is in front of us, there is not much to change. It is when we look at the big question and begin to question that we notice there are ways to improve our wider practices.

I want to cover some touchier subjects because we have been taught not to talk about them. The ugly side of history, racism, and the next few topics I discuss are supposed to make you feel a little icky. Icky means that there is room for discussion and growth.

The Curious Case of Education: Wow. If you had not thought critically about our education system before reading this chapter, you have now. In addition to reading about education, we dabbled in politics, funding, and the various types of capital that are not simply money. This piece highlights many postmodernist critiques; however, let us explore one question and go from there.

Bryan mentioned that his degree from UNC Asheville was different than a degree at Harvard because society puts different emphasis on these universities. I can agree with this, and I bet you can too. If the purpose of higher education is meant to prepare students to become effective members of society, what makes one degree better or worse than another?

Let us take a minute to consider that some schools are known for certain programs. If you want to go to school for teaching, you could say that a school mainly focused on its teaching program would be worth more on face value than a school known for its acting program. You want to be a teacher, not an actor. If we were to just look at universities in general and not based on a specific program, you could argue that the college's reputation is made up from the students who go there, which is a postmodern critique. People who have graduated from well-ranked private schools likely raise kids similar to them, as highlighted by social reproduction that was explored in Bryan and Fuller's chapter. The same goes for parents of students who went to an average public university; they are more inclined to raise similar students (so the theory goes). So, if universities are actually recipients of their previous students, can they ever change significantly? If colleges are ranked based on the education they provide, and if that education depends on the students, are we not, in fact, ranking the students who choose to attend those colleges? Society has put a rank on teenagers before they even have a chance to make their mark.

The next question is, is this fair? Think about it, and then *bam*, you have started your own critique.

Foundations of Social Research: Together, Bissell and Boland were able to explain and define the steps of a research project through a few examples. They showed you how important not only the thought process behind your initial ideas are but that even things like data collection and the validity of your sources are crucial steps to the overall process.

People use the internet to form their opinions in ways that no other form of information has been used before. The expansion of the internet has brought along many positives and negatives. One negative, not directly caused by the internet, is that people swear by the information they read online without checking into the sources. I have been in many situations where people joke, "Well I read it on the internet, so it must be true, right?" Wrong. As much as we make fun of it, it is very much an accepted idea. A postmodern critique of the internet is that the internet coupled with a desire for instant answers causes many people to accept what they read at face value, which is bad.

For twelve-plus years, we, as students, have been taught not to read Wikipedia, and yet I bet each and every one of us has. Why? Because it is easy and because it is a top search result. A more academic, and better, way would be to read a few of the sources that were cited in the references section. It takes minimal effort to click on three or even just two of the sources listed. You could take a completely different route and use your favorite search engine to find a few credible sources if you did not want to read the reference section on Wikipedia.

By diving further into a website or a study's data, you are becoming a better researcher and a more informed public intellectual. In an earlier chapter, we saw how important it was not to repeat someone else's opinion without questioning and actively thinking about it. Here, it is important not to randomly cite data or research you find without understanding how it was collected. By wondering about researchers' data collection methods or their testable research question, you help to put yourself in their shoes. This can only lead to a deeper understanding of the topic you are looking up.

Becoming a Public Intellectual: During his portion of the story, Yeganian focuses on our generation's access to technology. He thinks that while it is inherently better, it is up to us to use that information to become informed and respectful citizens. He points out the 2016 election, the incidents at Drake University, and discourse of various types to elaborate on the ways we owe it to ourselves to become more aware of our surroundings. In this case, it is clear the modern approach would be to say that the increase of access to information is good. The postmodern critique would be asking if it truly is good.

In addition to technology, we also have an increase of access to others' opinions and ways to express our opinions. Twitter is be a prime example. It is a medium where people can share thoughts, opinions, and facts, if you distinguish the difference. People often screenshot and share tweets via other mediums. Recently, a high-ranking government official "tweeted" about his opinion of Puerto Rico and the devastation caused by Hurricane Maria. I put "tweet" in quotation marks because it turns out the tweet my friend showed me was fake. His other friend had posted on Facebook and was ranting about it. My friend found out it was fake because he visited the politician's Twitter page to see if it was there, and it was not. We see that this access to technology and fake information crossed many boundaries: Facebook, Twitter, and face-to-face interaction. Did this access create any good? I would say no. In fact, it caused anguish for the person ranting on Facebook, it caused my friend to look up the validity of the tweet, and it wasted our time while we talked about it during class.

This example shows that access to technology did not do us any good. A postmodern view would be that the gain from access to information depends on the validity of the information and how we choose to act on that information. Not only do you have to be a consumer of information, you must be a smart consumer of information. This circles back to checking the sources, questioning the message of the research, and making sure you know what is going on before forming your own critique.

Developing Identity and Agency as a Scholar: Perkins does a great job of tackling the two ideas of identity and agency through narrative. To rephrase each of these words, identity comprises the experiences you have each day that are woven into your story while agency is how you respond in each of those situations. Agency and identity are two topics that have been heavily disputed in postmodernism critiques. In fact, Perkins mentions this in her chapter. If you would like to read more on these topics, you may look at her reference section (which would make you a better researcher and public intellectual—see what I did there? I admit, I think I am clever sometimes). While she pointed out many examples, I want to explain the ideas again through a therapist example.

I think that therapists have a wonderful mission, and I have personally benefitted from therapy, so this is no rap on therapists. Therapists want to help people get "better". When we look at the word *better*, who determined what the definition of better is? Of course, we can look at the origin of the term and the history of its use, but what makes this the best version? Somewhere along the way, we decided as a society how a "normal" person should act. Cool. Then, we built ideas of how to get better, with therapy being one. Great. However, now would be a good time to sit down and think about where those ideas came from and why we have put those ideas on a pedestal.

If the person in therapy says they feel better in a session but then later realize they have other problems, are they still the same person they were in the session? This goes back to identity. We read that identity can be argued as a constantly changing perspective and that we act on these perspectives through our actions. I agree that our identity will never be the same as it was yesterday and that our agency may or may not always be aligned with our identity as situations occur. The only thing that matters for your development as a student is if you agree or not and why. I took the time to create the therapist example; see if you can identify where you see identity and agency interacting in your life. After this, you will have a third postmodern critique from this summary.

The ideas discussed in this book will not go away or decrease in importance as you go through your higher-level education experience. In fact, the longer you are in college, I bet you will see more of these principles in action like I have. Looking back on my freshman year, I would have liked to have had the opportunity to read this book because it would have helped develop my critical eye. Now that you have your critical eye, go out there and see what you can do; talk about icky subjects, be respectful of other's opinions, and always question, question, question.

CPSIA information can be obtained
at www.ICGtesting.com
Printed in the USA
LVHW050036190820
663559LV00012B/1841

9 781516 511115